Lord Chesterfield's Letters

To his Son and Godson, Selected

WITH INTRODUCTION, BIOGRAPHICAL SKETCH, AND NOTES

BY

HENRY H. BELFIELD, Ph. D.

Director of the Chicago Manual Training School

NEW YORK

MAYNARD, MERRILL, & CO.

29, 31 AND 33 EAST 19TH STREET

Copyright, 1897, by MAYNARD, MERRILL, & CO.

Contents

4 ## CONTENTS

Introduction

"SURELY it is of great use to a young man, before he starts out for a country full of mazes, windings, and turnings, to have at least a good map of it by some experienced traveler." Thus did the author of these Letters state their object : and in this spirit has this selection of them been prepared for the use of American youth.

For more than a century the Letters of Lord Chesterfield have commanded the admiration of lovers of English literature. "The Letters are brilliantly written—full of elegant wisdom, of keen wit, of admirable portrait painting, of exquisite observation and deduction. Viewed as compositions, they appear almost unrivaled as models for a serious epistolary style : clear, elegant, and terse, never straining at effect and yet never hurried into carelessness."—*Lord Mahon*. As literature, they have never been criticised : but their morality has been condemned as doubtful, or worse, and their perusal by the young has been regarded as having a tendency to debase, rather than to elevate. The answer to this charge has usually been "that the Letters reflected the morality of the age, and that their author only systematized and reduced to writing the principles of conduct by which, deliberately or unconsciously. the best and the worst of his contemporaries were governed."

While this is true of some of the letters, it is equally true that, in others, moral conduct is repeatedly and forcibly inculcated, but generally, it is to be regretted, from the lowest motive, selfishness. Lord Chesterfield advocates purity of character as many advocate honesty, because it is the best policy. Between his basis for a correct life, and the New Testament basis, there is a great gulf. Even the stoic Emperor, Marcus Aurelius, lives on a far higher plane. But that Lord Chesterfield does insist upon a moral life is recognized by the readers of his letters, though probably unsuspected by those who know him simply by his general reputation. In the Letter numbered XXX. in this volume, he says : "Your moral character must be not only pure, but, like Cæsar's wife, unsuspected. The

5

least speck or blemish upon it is fatal." " There is nothing so delicate
as your moral character, and nothing which it is your interest so
much to preserve pure." And he denounces those who believe, or
affect to believe, that there is no difference between " moral good
and evil," as " unaccountable wretches," "the devil's hypocrites."
His teaching, therefore, is not adverse to Christian morals: he
preaches morality, but on the ground of expediency. /He assumes
that his son has had no lack of Christian instruction : and he adds his
testimony, " as a man of the world," to the value of a good character
from a business point of view.   In a letter dated May 15, O. S. 1749
(not included in this volume), he says : " I am not now preaching to
you, like an old fellow, upon either religious or moral texts : I am
persuaded you do not want the best instruction of that kind ; but
I am advising you as a friend, as a man of the world, as one who
would not have you old while you are young, but would have you
take all the pleasures that reason points out, and decency warrants."

.   .   .   .

" I will, therefore, suppose for argument's sake (for upon no other
account can it be supposed) that all the vices above mentioned were
perfectly innocent in themselves : they would still degrade, vilify, and
sink those who practiced them ; would obstruct their rising in the
world, by debasing their characters ; and give them a low turn of
mind and manners, absolutely inconsistent with their making any
figure in upper life, and great business."
Chesterfield was a life-long admirer of Voltaire, whom he introduced to his friends in England ; but he did not hesitate to write thus
to the great Frenchman :
" I strongly doubt whether it is permissible for a man to write
against the worship and belief of his country, even if he be fully persuaded of its error, on account of the terrible trouble and disorder it
might cause ; but I am sure it is in no wise allowable to attack the
foundations of true morality, and to break unnecessary bonds which
are already too weak to keep men in the path of duty."
It seems therefore to the present editor that the letters included in
this volume are instructive and valuable to the young, as the testimony to the necessity of purity of character given by a man who
knew thoroughly the moral rottenness of a dissolute age.
To the other charge made against the Letters, that they insist " too
much on manners and graces, instead of more solid acquirements,"
Lord Mahon replies that it " is certainly erroneous, and arises only

from the idea and expectation of finding a general system of education in letters intended solely for the improvement of one man. Young Stanhope was sufficiently inclined to study, and imbued with knowledge ; the difficulty lay in his awkward address and indifference to pleasing. It is against these faults, therefore, and these faults only, that Chesterfield points his battery of eloquence. Had he found his son, on the contrary, a graceful but superficial trifler, his letters would, no doubt, have urged, with equal zeal, how vain are all accomplishments, when not supported by sterling information. In one word, he intended to write for Mr. Philip Stanhope, and not for any other person. And yet, even after this great deduction from general utility, it was still the opinion of a most eminent man, no friend of Chesterfield, and no proficient in the graces—the opinion of Dr. Johnson, ' Take out the immorality, and the letters should be put into the hands of every young gentleman.' "

It should be remembered that the Letters were not written for publication, nor with any expectation of their being read except by the son to whom the fond and anxious father opened his heart. By his letters is Lord Chesterfield remembered ; while his prominence in political and literary circles is forgotten.

The constant recurrence of foreign words and phrases illustrates not only the fashion which then prevailed, of making frequent use of such quotations, but the fact, also, that a knowledge of both ancient and modern languages was very common among educated Englishmen. Several of Lord Chesterfield's letters, to his son and to his godson, were written in French, others in Latin.

Biographical Sketch

PHILIP DORMER STANHOPE, fourth Earl of CHESTERFIELD, was born in London, in 1694, the son of Philip Stanhope, the third Earl, and Elizabeth Savile, daughter of the Marquis of Halifax. He spent two years at Cambridge (1712–13), where he seems to have studied ancient and modern languages, history, and oratory. As a boy he had formed the habit of early rising, which he always maintained : and by a systematic use of his time he was able to accomplish much. He regarded his college, Trinity Hall, "infinitely the best in the University ; for it is the smallest, and filled with lawyers who have lived in the world, and know how to behave." His immaturity, not to say weakness, of character is shown by his confession to his son, years afterward, that when he first went to the University at eighteen years of age, "he drank and smoked, notwithstanding the aversion he had to wine and tobacco, only because he thought it genteel, and that it made him look like a man."

At the age of twenty he left Cambridge for the conventional tour on the Continent, visiting Holland, Belgium, and Paris. He entered the House of Commons in 1715, and made his maiden speech on the impeachment of the Duke of Ormond : and, on its conclusion, was informed that he had rendered himself liable to a heavy fine for addressing the House before he had attained his majority. Although he afterward took frequent part in the debates of the House, his oratory never made the deep impression that it did in the House of Lords, in which he took his seat on the death of his father in 1726. Here his oratorical powers at once commanded attention, and established his reputation as one of the most eloquent speakers of his age. Horace Walpole, who had heard Pitt, Pulteney, Windham, and Carteret, as well as his own father, declared that the finest speech he ever heard was one delivered by Lord Chesterfield. But this is probably an overestimate.

On the accession of George II., in 1727, Lord Chesterfield became ambassador to The Hague, where he remained till 1732, distinguishing himself by his tact, judgment, and dexterity. His services were rewarded by his being made a Knight of the Garter, and Lord High Steward. Here, at The Hague, in 1732, was born Philip Stanhope, the son to whom the famous letters were written.

On his return to England he resumed his seat in the House of Lords, in which he was the acknowledged leader of the opposition for several years. He was sent the second time to The Hague in 1744 ; and succeeded so well in his mission that he was given the Lord-Lieutenancy of Ireland, a post long coveted by him.

"Short as it was, Chesterfield's Irish administration was of great service to his country, and is unquestionably that part of his political life which does him most honor. To have conceived and carried out a policy which, with certain reservations, Burke himself might have originated and owned, is indeed no small title to regard. The earl showed himself finely capable in practice as in theory, vigorous and tolerant, a man to be feared, and a leader to be followed ; he took the government entirely into his own hands, repressed the jobbery traditional to the office, established schools and manufactures, and at once conciliated and kept in check the Orange and Popish factions."— *Encyc. Brit.* "It was he who first, since the revolution, had made that office a post of active exertion. Only a few years before, the Earl of Shrewsbury had given as a reason for accepting it, that it was a place where a man had business enough to hinder him from falling asleep, and not enough to keep him awake. Chesterfield, on the contrary, left nothing undone, nor for others to do. . . . So able were the measures of Chesterfield ; so clearly did he impress upon the public mind that his moderation was not weakness, nor his clemency cowardice, but that, to quote his own words, 'his hand should be as heavy as Cromwell's' upon them if they once forced him to raise it ; so well did he know how to scare the timid, while con- ciliating the generous, that this alarming period [1745] passed over with a degree of tranquillity such as Ireland has not often displayed even in orderly and settled times."—*Lord Mahon.*

In 1746 he became Secretary of State for Ireland, from which position he retired in 1748, declining the dukedom offered him by George II.

In 1751, assisted by Lord Macclesfield and the mathematician Bradley, he contributed largely to the reform of the calendar. He thus describes to his son his share in the work : "I have of late been a sort of *astronome malgré moi* [an astronomer in spite of myself] by bringing last Monday into the House of Lords a bill for reforming our present calendar, and taking the New Style. Upon which occasion I was obliged to talk some astronomical jargon, of which I did not understand one word, but got it by heart, and spoke it by rote from a master. I wished that I had known a little more of it myself ; and so much I would have you know."

This was his last important public act. Lord Chesterfield's relations with Dr. Johnson will always be remembered : and are here presented in the diction of Lord Macaulay, and of Johnson himself.

" The prospectus of the Dictionary he [Dr. Johnson] addressed to the Earl of Chesterfield. Chesterfield had long been celebrated for the politeness of his manners, the brilliancy of his wit, and the delicacy of his taste. He was acknowledged to be the finest speaker in the House of Lords. He had recently governed Ireland, at a momentous conjuncture, with eminent firmness, wisdom, and humanity, and he had since become Secretary of State. He received Johnson's homage with the most winning affability, and requited it with a few guineas, bestowed doubtless in a very graceful manner, but was by no means desirous to see all his carpets blacked with the London mud, and his soups and wines thrown to right and left over the gowns of fine ladies and the waistcoats of fine gentlemen, by an absent, awkward scholar, who gave strange starts and uttered strange growls, who dressed like a scarecrow and ate like a cormorant. During some time Johnson continued to call on his patron, but, after being repeatedly told by the porter that his lordship was not at home, took the hint, and ceased to present himself at the inhospitable door. . . . It had been generally supposed that this great work would be dedicated to the eloquent and accomplished nobleman to whom the prospectus had been addressed. He well knew the value of such a compliment ; and therefore, when the day of publication drew near, he exerted himself to soothe, by a show of zealous and at the same time of delicate and judicious kindness, the pride which he had so cruelly wounded. Since *The Rambler* had ceased to appear, the town had been entertained by a journal called *The World*, to which many men of high rank and fashion contributed. In two successive numbers of *The World*, the Dictionary was, to use the modern phrase, puffed with wonderful skill. The writings of Johnson were warmly praised. It was proposed that he should be invested with the authority of a dictator, nay, of a pope, over our language, and that his decisions about the meaning and the spelling of words should be received as final. His two folios, it was said, would of course be bought by everybody who could afford to buy them. It was soon known that these papers were written by Chesterfield. But the just resentment of Johnson was not to be appeased. In a letter written with singular energy and dignity of thought and language, he repelled the tardy advances of his patron. The Dictionary came forth without a dedication."

The following is the letter above described, which did not see the light, however, till 1781.

To the Right Honorable the Earl of Chesterfield.

February 7, 1755.

MY LORD : I have been lately informed, by the proprietor of *The World*, that papers, in which my Dictionary is recommended to the public, were written by your Lordship. To be so distinguished is an honor which, being very little accustomed to favors from the great, I know not well how to receive, or in what terms to acknowledge.

When, upon some slight encouragement, I first visited your Lordship, I was overpowered, like the rest of mankind, by the enchantment of your address, and could not forbear to wish that I might boast myself *Le vainqueur du vainqueur de la terre :*—that I might obtain that regard for which I saw the world contending ; but I found my attendance so little encouraged, that neither pride nor modesty would suffer me to continue it. When I had once addressed your Lordship in public, I had exhausted all the art of pleasing which a retired and uncourtly scholar can possess. I had done all that I could, and no man is well pleased to have his all neglected, be it ever so little.

Seven years, my Lord, have now passed, since I waited in your outward rooms, or was repulsed from your door ; during which time I have been pushing on my work through difficulties, of which it is useless to complain, and have brought it, at last, to the verge of publication, without one act of assistance, one word of encouragement, or one smile of favor. Such treatment I did not expect, for I never had a patron before.

The Shepherd of Virgil grew at last acquainted with Love, and found him a native of the rocks.

Is not a patron, my Lord, one who looks with unconcern on a man struggling for life in the water, and, when he has reached ground, encumbers him with help ? The notice which you have been pleased to take of my labors, had it been early had been kind ; but it has been delayed till I am indifferent, and cannot enjoy it ; till I am solitary, and cannot impart it ; till I am known, and do not want it. I hope it is no very cynical asperity not to confess obligations where no benefit has been received, or to be unwilling that the public should consider me as owing that to a patron, which Providence has enabled me to do for myself.

Having carried on my work thus far with so little obligation to any favorer of learning, I shall not be disappointed though I should conclude it, if it be possible, with less : for I have been long wakened from that dream of hope, in which I once boasted myself with so much exaltation, my Lord,

Your Lordship's most humble,

Most obedient servant,

SAM. JOHNSON.

During the latter part of Chesterfield's life he was afflicted with deafness.   This caused him to withdraw from public life, and devote himself to his books and his pen.   Blindness followed.   His wit did not forsake him.   " Tyrawley and I," he said, " have been dead these two years, but we don't choose to have it known."   Nor did his fine manners fail him.   His last words were " Give Dayrolles a chair."   He died March 24, 1773.

Chesterfield married, in 1733, Melusina von Schulemberg, a daughter of George I.   Philip Stanhope, to whom the Letters were addressed, had died in 1768 ; and Chesterfield made his godson, also named Philip Stanhope, but a distant relative, the heir to his title and estates.

Lord Chesterfield's Letters To His Son

Letter I

THE VALUE OF HISTORY.

November the 20th, 1739.

DEAR BOY: As you are now reading the Roman History, I hope you do it with that care and attention which it deserves. The utility of History consists principally in the examples it gives us of the virtues 5 and vices of those who have gone before us: upon which we ought to make the proper observations. History animates and excites us to the love and the practice of virtue; by showing us the regard and veneration that was always paid to great and virtuous 10 men, in the times in which they lived, and the praise and glory with which their names are perpetuated, and transmitted down to our times. The Roman History furnishes more examples of virtue and magnanimity, or greatness of mind, than any other. It 15 was a common thing to see their Consuls and Dictators (who, you know, were their chief Magistrates) taken from the plow, to lead their armies against their enemies; and, after victory, returning to their plow again, and passing the rest of their lives in modest 20 retirement: a retirement more glorious, if possible,

than the victories that preceded it! Many of their
greatest men died so poor, that they were buried at
the expense of the public. Curius, who had no
money of his own, refused a great sum that the Sam-
5 nites offered him, saying, that he saw no glory in having money himself, but in commanding those that
had. Cicero relates it thus: " *Curio ad focum sedenti
magnum auri pondus Samnites cum attulissent, repudiati
ab eo sunt. Non enim aurum habere præclarum sibi*
10 *videri, sed iis, qui haberent aurum, imperare.*" And
Fabricius, who had often commanded the Roman
armies, and as often triumphed over their enemies,
was found by his fireside, eating those roots and herbs
which he had planted and cultivated himself in his
15 own field. Seneca tells it thus: *Fabricius ad focum
cœnat illas ipsas radices, quas, in agro repurgando, tri-
umphalis Senex vulsit.* Scipio, after a victory he had
obtained in Spain, found among the prisoners a young
Princess of extreme beauty, who, he was informed,
20 was soon to have been married to a man of quality of
that country. He ordered her to be entertained and
attended with the same care and respect, as if she had
been in her father's house; and, as soon as he could
find her lover, he gave her to him, and added to her
25 portion the money that her father had brought for

---

[3] **Curius**, M. Dentatus, who defeated Pyrrhus in 275 B. C.

[7] **Curio** . . . . **imperare.** Translated in lines 3 to 7.

[11] **Fabricius**, Caius. Like his contemporary, Dentatus, he refused large gifts
offered by the Samnite ambassadors, and died poor.

[16] **Seneca**, Lucius Annæus. (3 B. C.-65 A. D.) A Roman philosopher, tutor
of Nero, and " the most brilliant figure of his time."

[16] **Fabricius** . . . . **vulsit.** Translated in lines 10 to 15.

[17] **Scipio** Africanus, Publius Cornelius. (B. C. 234-183.) Of a noble Roman
family of the Cornelian *gens*, three members of which were particularly celebrated
for their valor, patriotism, and generalship in the Punic wars.

her ransom. Valerius Maximus says, *Eximiæ formæ virginem accersitis parentibus, et sponso inviolatam tradidit, et Juvenis, et Cœlebs, et Victor.* This was a most glorious example of moderation, continence, and generosity, which gained him the hearts of all 5 the people of Spain; and made them say, as Livy tells us, *Venisse Diis simillimum juvenem, vincentem omnia, cum armis, tum benignitate, ac beneficiis.*

Such are the rewards that always crown virtue; and such the characters that you should imitate, if you 10 would be a great and a good man, which is the only way to be a happy one! Adieu.

Letter II

THE AMBITIONS OF BOYS

DEAR BOY: I send you here a few more Latin roots, though I am not sure that you will like my roots so well as those that grow in your garden; how- 15 ever, if you will attend to them, they may save you a great deal of trouble. These few will naturally point out many others to your own observation; and enable you, by comparison, to find out most derived and compound words, when once you know the origi- 20 nal root of them. You are old enough now to make observations upon what you learn; which, if you

---

[1] **Valerius Maximus.** A compiler of historical anecdotes, who lived in the reign of Tiberius.

[1] **Eximiæ . . . . Victor.** Freely rendered in lines 21 to 25, p. 14.

[6] **Livy.** (59 B. C.-17 A. D.) A noted Roman historian.

[7] **Venisse . . . . beneficiis.** "Scipio came in the likeness of the gods, overcoming everything with his army, his generosity, and his good deeds."

would be pleased to do, you cannot imagine how
much time and trouble it would save you.   Remember, you are now very near nine years old; an age at
which all boys ought to know a great deal, but you,
5 particularly, a great deal more, considering the care
and pains that have been employed about you; and if
you do not answer those expectations, you will lose
your character; which is the most mortifying thing
that can happen to a generous mind.   Everybody
10 has ambition, of some kind or other, and is vexed
when that ambition is disappointed: the difference is,
that the ambition of silly people is a silly and mistaken
ambition; and the ambition of people of sense is a
right and commendable one.   For instance; the
15 ambition of a silly boy, of your age, would be to have
fine clothes, and money to throw away in idle follies;
which, you plainly see, would be no proofs of merit
in him, but only of folly in his parents, in dressing
him out like a jackanapes, and giving him money to
20 play the fool with.   Whereas a boy of good sense
places his ambition in excelling other boys of his own
age, and even older, in virtue and knowledge.   His
glory is in being known always to speak the truth, in
showing good-nature and compassion, in learning
25 quicker, and applying himself more than other boys.
These are real proofs of merit in him, and consequently proper objects of ambition; and will acquire
him a solid reputation and character.   This holds
true in men, as well as in boys; the ambition of a silly
30 fellow will be, to have a fine equipage, a fine house,
and fine clothes; things which anybody, that has as
much money, may have as well as he; for they are
all to be bought: but the ambition of a man of sense

and honor is, to be distinguished by a character and reputation of knowledge, truth, and virtue; things which are not to be bought, and that can only be acquired by a good head and a good heart. Such was the ambition of the Lacedæmonians and the 5 Romans, when they made the greatest figure; and such, I hope, yours will always be. Adieu.

Letter III

GOOD BREEDING

WEDNESDAY.

DEAR BOY: You behaved yourself so well at Mr. Boden's last Sunday, that you justly deserve commen- 10 dation: besides, you encourage me to give you some rules of politeness and good breeding, being persuaded that you will observe them. Know, then, that as learning, honor, and virtue are absolutely necessary to gain you the esteem and admiration 15 of mankind; politeness and good breeding are equally necessary to make you welcome and agreeable in conversation and common life. Great talents, such as honor, virtue, learning, and parts, are above the generality of the world; who neither possess them 20 themselves, nor judge of them rightly in others: but all people are judges of the lesser talents, such as civility, affability, and an obliging, agreeable address and manner; because they feel the good effects of them, as making society easy and pleasing. Good 25 sense must, in many cases, determine good breeding; because the same thing that would be civil at one time, and to one person, may be quite otherwise at

another time, and to another person; but there are some general rules of good breeding, that hold always true, and in all cases. As, for example, it is always extremely rude to answer only Yes, or No, to any-
5 body, without adding, Sir, my Lord, or Madam, according to the quality of the person you speak to; as, in French, you must always say, *Monsieur, Milord, Madame*, and *Mademoiselle*. I suppose you know that every married woman is, in French, *Madame*, and
10 every unmarried one is *Mademoiselle*. It is likewise extremely rude not to give the proper attention, and a civil answer, when people speak to you; or to go away, or be doing something else, while they are speaking to you; for that convinces them that you
15 despise them, and do not think it worth your while to hear or answer what they say. I dare say I need not tell you how rude it is to take the best place in a room, or to seize immediately upon what you like at table, without offering first to help others, as if you con-
20 sidered nobody but yourself. On the contrary, you should always endeavor to procure all the conveniences you can to the people you are with. Besides being civil, which is absolutely necessary, the perfection of good breeding is, to be civil with ease, and in
25 a gentlemanlike manner. For this, you should observe the French people, who excel in it, and whose politeness seems as easy and natural as any other part of their conversation. Whereas the English are often awkward in their civilities, and, when they mean
30 to be civil, are too much ashamed to get it out. But, pray, do you remember never to be ashamed of doing what is right: you would have a great deal of reason to be ashamed if you were not civil: but what

reason can you have to be ashamed of being civil? And why not say a civil and an obliging thing as easily and as naturally as you would ask what o'clock it is? This kind of bashfulness, which is justly called, by the French, *mauvaise honte*, is the distinguishing 5 character of an English booby; who is frightened out of his wits, when people of fashion speak to him; and when he is to answer them, blushes, stammers, can hardly get out what he would say, and becomes really ridiculous, from a groundless fear of being 10 laughed at: whereas a real well-bred man would speak to all the Kings in the world, with as little concern, and as much ease, as he would speak to you.

Remember, then, that to be civil, and to be civil with ease (which is properly called good breeding), 15 is the only way to be beloved, and well received in company; that to be ill-bred, and rude, is intolerable, and the way to be kicked out of company; and that to be bashful is to be ridiculous. As I am sure you will mind and practice all this, I expect that when you 20 are *novennis*, you will not only be the best scholar but the best-bred boy in England of your age. Adieu.

Letter IV

THE ATHENIAN OSTRACISM *

BATH, October 14, 1740.
DEAR BOY: Since I have recommended to you to think upon subjects, and to consider things in their 25

---

* Mauvaise honte. False shame or modesty.
21 Novennis. Nine years old.
* This letter, a request to assist the writer in forming his opinions, is delicate flattery, designed to lead the boy into the habit of thinking on important subjects.

various lights and circumstances, I am persuaded
you have made such a progress that I shall sometimes desire your opinion upon difficult points, in
order to form my own.   For instance, though I have
5 in general a great veneration for the manners and
customs of the ancients, yet I am in some doubt
whether the Ostracism of the Athenians was either
just or prudent, and should be glad to be determined
by your opinion. You know very well that the
10 Ostracism was the method of banishing those whose
distinguished virtue made them popular, and consequently (as the Athenians thought) dangerous to the
public liberty.   And, if six hundred citizens of Athens
gave in the name of any one Athenian, written upon an
15 oyster-shell (from whence it is called ostracism) that
man was banished Athens for ten years.   On one hand,
it is certain that a free people cannot be too careful or
jealous of their liberty; and it is certain, too, that the
love of applause of mankind will always attend a man
20 of eminent and distinguished virtue; and, consequently, they are more likely to give up their liberties
to such a one, than to another of less merit.   But
then, on the other hand, it seems extraordinary to
discourage virtue upon any account, since it is only
25 by virtue that any society can flourish and be considerable.   There are many more arguments, on each
side of the question, which will naturally occur to
you; and, when you have considered them well, I
desire you will write me your opinion whether the
30 Ostracism was a right or a wrong thing, and your
reasons for being of that opinion.   Let nobody help
you; but give me exactly your own sentiments, and
your own reasons, whatever they are.

Letter V

THE USE OF OTHERS' THOUGHTS: PROPER USE OF
EPITHETS

THURSDAY.

DEAR BOY: You will seldom hear from me, without
an admonition to think. All you learn, and all you
can read, will be of little use, if you do not think and
reason upon it yourself. One reads, to know other 5
people's thoughts; but if we take them upon trust,
without examining them and comparing them with
our own, it is really living upon other people's goods.
To know the thoughts of others is of use, because it
suggests thoughts to one's self, and helps to form a 10
judgment; but to repeat other people's thoughts,
without considering whether they are right or wrong,
is the talent only of a parrot, or at most a player.

If *Night* were given you as a subject to compose
upon, you would do very well to look what the best 15
authors have said upon it, in order to help your own
invention; but then you must think of it afterward
yourself, and express it in your own manner, or else
you would be at best but a plagiary. A plagiary is a
man who steals other people's thoughts, and puts 20
them off for his own. You would find, for example,
the following account of Night in Virgil:

" It was now night, and the weary ones were enjoying sweet slumber
   Through all the earth ; the woods and wild waves were at rest from
      their raging, 25
   While in the midst of their orbits the stars glide on in their
      courses,

---

²² **Night in Virgil.** Lord Chesterfield quotes the original (Æneid, IV. 522-528)
for which a translation by Howland is substituted.

> While every field is hushed, the flocks and the birds of gay plum-
> age,
> Those that inhabit the liquid lakes, or the rough fields and
> thickets ;
> 5 Through the deep silence of night, these all are buried in slumber,
> Soothing their anxious cares, and their hearts forgetful of sorrow."

Here you see the effects of Night; that it brings
rest to men when they are wearied with the labors of
the day; that the stars move in their regular courses;
10 that flocks and birds repose themselves, and enjoy
the quiet of the night. This, upon examination, you
would find to be all true; but then, upon consideration, too, you would find that it is not all that is to
be said upon Night, and many more qualities and
15 effects of night would occur to you. As for instance,
though night is in general the time for quiet and repose, yet it is often the time for the commission and
security of crimes, such as robberies, murders, and
violations, which generally seek the advantage of
20 darkness, as favorable for the escapes of the guilty.
Night, too, though it brings rest and refreshment to
the innocent and virtuous, brings disquiet and horror
to the guilty. The consciousness of their crimes
torments them and denies them sleep and quiet. You
25 might, from these reflections, consider what would be
the proper epithets to give to Night; as, for example,
if you were to represent Night in its most pleasing
shape, as procuring quiet and refreshment from
labor and toil, you might call it the *friendly* Night,
30 the *silent* Night, the *welcome* Night, the *peaceful* Night;
but if, on the contrary, you were to represent it as
inviting to the commission of crimes, you would call
it the *guilty* Night, the *conscious* Night, the *horrid*

Night, with many other epithets that carry along with them the idea of horror and guilt; for an epithet, to be proper, must always be adapted (that is, suited) to the circumstances of the person or thing to which it is given. Thus, Virgil, who generally gives Æneas 5 the epithet of *pious*, because of his piety to the gods and his duty to his father, calls him *Dux* Æneas where he represents him making love to Dido, as a proper epithet for him in that situation: because making love becomes a general much better than a man of singular 10 piety.

Lay aside, for a few minutes, the thoughts of play, and think of this seriously.

Amoto quæramus seria ludo.

Adieu! 15

Letter VI

THE EVILS OF AWKWARDNESS

Spa, the 25th July, N. S. 1741.

DEAR BOY: I have often told you in my former letters (and it is most certainly true) that the strictest and most scrupulous honor and virtue can alone make you esteemed and valued by mankind; that 20 parts and learning can alone make you admired and celebrated by them; but that the possession of lesser talents was most absolutely necessary toward making you liked, beloved, and sought after in private life. Of these lesser talents, good breeding is the principal 25 and most necessary one, not only as it is very impor-

---

⁷ Dux : a leader or general.

¹⁴ Amoto . . . . ludo. Horace, Satires, I. 1, 27. " Let us cease our play and seek serious matters."

tant in itself, but as it adds great luster to the more
solid advantages both of the heart and the mind. I
have often touched upon good breeding to you before,
so that this letter shall be upon the next necessary
5 qualification to it, which is a genteel, easy manner and
carriage, wholly free from those odd tricks, ill habits,
and awkwardnesses which even many very worthy and
sensible people have in their behavior. However
trifling a genteel manner may sound, it is of very great
10 consequence toward pleasing in private life, especially
the women, which, one time or other, you will think
worth pleasing; and I have known many a man, from
his awkwardness, give people such a dislike of him
at first, that all his merit could not get the better of
15 it afterward.   Whereas a genteel manner prepossesses
people in your favor, bends them toward you, and
makes them wish to like you.   Awkwardness can proceed but from two causes—either from not having
kept good company, or from not having attended
20 to it. As for your keeping good company, I will
take care of that; do you take care to observe their
ways and manners, and to form your own upon them.
Attention is absolutely necessary for this, as indeed it
is for everything else, and a man without attention
25 is not fit to live in the world. When an awkward
fellow first comes into a room, it is highly probable
that his sword gets between his legs and throws him
down, or makes him stumble, at least.   When he has
recovered this accident, he goes and places himself
30 in the very place of the whole room where he should
not; there he soon lets his hat fall down, and in taking

27 His sword. In Lord Chesterfield's time, a dress suit included a dress
sword.

it up again, throws down his cane; in recovering his
cane, his hat falls a second time; so that he is a
quarter of an hour before he is in order again. If
he drinks tea or coffee he certainly scalds his mouth,
and lets either the cup or the saucer fall, and spills 5
the tea or coffee in his breeches. At dinner his awkwardness distinguishes itself particularly, as he has
more to do: there he holds his knife, fork, and spoon
differently from other people; eats with his knife to
the great danger of his mouth; picks his teeth with 10
his fork, and puts his spoon, which has been in his
throat twenty times, into the dishes again. If he is
to carve, he can never hit the joint, but, in his vain
efforts to cut through the bone, scatters the sauce in
everybody's face. He generally daubs himself with 15
soup and grease, though his napkin is commonly
stuck through a botton-hole and tickles his chin.
When he drinks he infallibly coughs in his glass, and
besprinkles the company. His hands are troublesome to him when he has not something in them, 20
and he does not know where to put them; but they
are in perpetual motion between his bosom and his
breeches: he does not wear his clothes, and, in short,
does nothing, like other people. All this, I own, is
not in any degree criminal; but it is highly disagree- 25
able and ridiculous in company, and ought most carefully to be avoided by whoever desires to please.

From this account of what you should not do, you
may easily judge what you should do; and a due
attention to the manners of people of fashion, and 30
who have seen the world, will make it habitual and
familiar to you.

There is, likewise, an awkwardness of expression

and words, most carefully to be avoided; such as false
English, bad pronunciation, old sayings, and common proverbs; which are so many proofs of having
kept bad and low company.   For example; if, instead
5 of saying that tastes are different, and that every man
has his own peculiar one, you should let off a proverb,
and say, That what is one man's meat is another
man's poison; or else, Everyone as they like, as the
good man said when he kissed his cow; everybody
10 would be persuaded that you had never kept company
with anybody above footmen and housemaids.

Attention will do all this; and without attention
nothing is to be done: want of attention, which is
really want of thought, is either folly or madness.
15 You should not only have attention to everything,
but a quickness of attention, so as to observe, at once,
all the people in the room, their motions, their looks,
and their words, and yet without staring at them,
and seeming to be an observer.   This quick and
20 unobserved observation is of infinite advantage in life,
and is to be acquired with care; and, on the contrary,
what is called absence, which is a thoughtlessness,
and want of attention about what is doing, makes
a man so like either a fool or a madman, that for
25 my part I see no real difference.   A fool never has
thought; a madman has lost it; and an absent man
is, for the time, without it.   Adieu.

Letter VII

A SEVERE REPROOF *

DUBLIN, January the 25th, 1745.

DEAR BOY: As there are now four mails due from England, one of which, at least, will, I suppose, bring me a letter from` you, I take this opportunity of acknowledging it beforehand, that you may not accuse 5 me (as you once or twice have done) of negligence. I am very glad to find, by your letter which I am to receive, that you are determined to apply yourself seriously to your business; to attend to what you learn, in order to learn it well; and to reflect and reason 10 upon what you have learned, that your learning may be of use to you. These are very good resolutions, and I applaud you mightily for them. Now for your last letter, which I have received. You rebuke me very severely for not knowing, or at least not remem- 15 bering, that you have been some time in the fifth form. Here, I confess, I am at a loss what to say for myself; for, on the one hand, I own it is not probable that you would not, at the time, have communicated an event of that importance to me; and, 20 on the other hand, it is not likely that, if you had informed me of it, I could have forgotten it. You say that it happened six months ago; in which, with all due submission to you, I apprehend you are mistaken, because that must have been before I left Eng- 25 land, which I am sure it was not; and it does not

---

* This letter was written while Lord Chesterfield was Lord-Lieutenant of Ireland.

appear, in any of your original manuscripts, that it
happened since.   May not this possibly proceed from
the oscitancy of the writer?   To this oscitancy of the
librarians, we owe so many mistakes, hiatuses, lacunæ,
5 etc., in ancient manuscripts.   It may here be necessary to explain to you the meaning of the *Oscitantes
librarii;* which, I believe, you will easily take.   These
persons (before printing was invented) transcribed
the works of authors, sometimes for their own profit,
10 but oftener (as they were generally slaves) for the
profit of their masters.   In the first case, dispatch,
more than accuracy, was their object; for the faster
they wrote the more they got: in the latter case
(observe this), as it was a task imposed on them,
15 which they did not dare to refuse, they were *idle, careless, and incorrect; not giving themselves the trouble to
read over what they had written.*   The celebrated
Atticus kept a great number of these transcribing
slaves, and got great sums of money by their labors.
20   But, to return now to your fifth form, from whence
I have strayed, it may be, too long; Pray what do you
do in that country?   Be so kind as to give me a
description of it. What Latin and Greek books do you
read there? Are your exercises exercises of invention?
25 or do you still put the bad English of the psalms into

Oscitancy. Laziness.

Librarians. Copyists.

Lacunæ. Gaps, or defects.

Oscitantes librarii. Lazy scribes.

18 **Atticus.**   T. Pomponius. (B. C. 109–32.)   Called Atticus from his long
residence in Athens, and his familiarity with Greek literature.   A friend of Cicero,
and a lover of books.   He owned "transcribing slaves, and book-binders, also."
Cicero thanks him for the services of two such slaves, who put Cicero's library in
good repair.   For an interesting chapter on libraries in ancient Rome, see Lan-
ciani's *Ancient Rome in the Light of Recent Discoveries.*

bad Latin, and only change the shape of Latin verse, from long to short, and from short to long? People do not improve, singly, by traveling, but by the observations they make, and by keeping good company where they do travel. So I hope, in your trav- 5 els, through the fifth form, you keep company with Horace and Cicero, among the Romans; and Homer and Xenophon, among the Greeks; and that you are got out of the worst company in the world, the Greek epigrams. Martial has wit, and is worth your look- 10 ing into sometimes; but I recommend the Greek epigrams to your supreme contempt. Good-night to you.

Letter VIII

TRIFLES

Dublin Castle, November the 19th, 1745.

Dear Boy: Now that the Christmas breaking up draws near, I have ordered Mr. Desnoyers to go to 15 you, during that time, to teach you to dance. I desire you will particularly attend to the graceful motion of your arms; which, with the manner of putting on your hat, and giving your hand, is all that a gentleman need attend to. Dancing is in itself a very trifling, 20 silly thing; but it is one of those established follies to which people of sense are sometimes obliged to

---

¹ **Latin verse.** The writing of Latin verses forms an important part of a pupil's duties in an English classical school.

¹⁰ **Martial.** M. Valerius Martialis. (A. D. 43-104.) A Roman poet who wrote his epigrams in Greek, in fourteen books. Roman scholars spoke and wrote Greek as well as Latin. Scipio Africanus (mentioned in Letter I.) spoke Greek and Latin with equal fluency, and wrote his memoirs in Greek. The Emperor Marcus Aurelius (A. D. 121-180) wrote his famous " Meditations " in Greek.

conform; and then they should be able to do it well.
And, though I would not have you a dancer, yet,
when you do dance, I would have you dance well,
as I would have you do everything you do well.
5 There is no one thing so trifling, but which (if it is
to be done at all) ought to be done well. And I have
often told you, that I wished you even played at pitch,
and cricket, better than any boy at Westminster. For
instance; dress is a very foolish thing; and yet it is
10 a very foolish thing for a man not to be well dressed,
according to his rank and way of life; and it is so far
from being a disparagement to any man's understanding, that it is rather a proof of it, to be as well dressed
as those whom he lives with: the difference in this
15 case, between a man of sense and a fop, is, that the

Westminster. One of the great English public schools, not *public* in the
American sense of *free*, but famous boarding schools for the sons of English
nobility and gentry. A fair idea of one of these schools at the time young Stanhope was a pupil at Westminster can be obtained from Professor Goldwin Smith's
description of Eton :

"At Eton the curriculum was in those days almost entirely classical, even
mathematics being taught out of school, and not as a regular part of the course.
Not only was the curriculum classical, but it was purely philological ; it did not
include ancient history or philosophy. Greek and Latin composition was the
exercise most valued, and in this great excellence, for boys, was certainly attained,
as an inspection of the *Musæ Etonenses* [Eton Muses] will show. There was little
effort on the part of the masters generally to exercise any moral influence over the
boys, to mold their character, or impress them with a sense of responsibility.
The boys were left to be a law to each other, and their standard was simply that of
the class from which they came : high in respect to manners and as to the point
of honor, but with regard to morality not so high. The discipline consisted in a
set of cast iron and sometimes antiquated regulations, to which everyone rendered
a sort of military obedience without asking the reason. It was enforced by rather
free use of corporal punishment, which, however, did not break the spirit of the
boys, or render them less sensitive about their honor, which they were ready
enough to avenge by fighting whenever they deemed themselves insulted."—
Educational Review, December, 1892. See also "Tom Brown's School Days at
Rugby." Lord Chesterfield appears to have had a poor opinion of Westminster
School, which, he says, "is undoubtedly the seat of illiberal manners and brutal
behavior."

fop values himself upon his dress; and the man of
sense laughs at it, at the same time that he knows
he must not neglect it.   There are a thousand foolish
customs of this kind, which not being criminal must
be complied with, and even cheerfully, by men of 5
sense.   Diogenes the Cynic was a wise man for
despising them; but a fool for showing it.   Be wiser
than other people, if you can; but do not tell them so.

It is a very fortunate thing for Sir Charles Hotham
to have fallen into the hands of one of your age, 10
experience, and knowledge of the world; I am persuaded you will take infinite care of him.   Good-
night.

Letter IX

INATTENTION: OBSERVATION

DUBLIN CASTLE, March 10, 1746.
SIR: I most thankfully acknowledge the honor of 15
two or three letters from you, since I troubled you
with my last; and am very proud of the repeated
instances you give me of your favor and protection,
which I shall endeavor to deserve.

I am very glad that you went to hear a trial in the 20
Court of King's Bench: and still more so, that you
made the proper animadversions upon the inattention of many of the people in the Court.   As you
observed very well the indecency of that inattention,
I am sure you will never be guilty of anything like 25

---

* **Diogenes the Cynic.**   (About B. C. 412–323.)   He despised even the comforts of life.

⁹ **Sir Charles Hotham.**   A young friend of Mr. Stanhope.

²¹ **Court of King's Bench.**   A court over which the king formerly presided.

it yourself. There is no surer sign in the world of
a little, weak mind than inattention. Whatever is
worth doing at all is worth doing well; and nothing
can be well done without attention. It is the sure
5 answer of a fool, when you ask him about anything
that was said or done where he was present, that
"truly he did not mind it." And why did not the
fool mind it? What else had he to do there but to
mind what he was doing? A man of sense sees, hears,
10 and retains everything that passes where he is. I
desire I may never hear you talk of not minding, nor
complain, as most fools do, of a treacherous memory.
Mind not only what people say but how they say it;
and if you have any sagacity, you may discover more
15 truth by your eyes than by your ears. People can
say what they will, but they cannot look just as they
will; and their looks frequently discover what their
words are calculated to conceal. Observe, therefore,
people's looks carefully when they speak, not only to
20 you, but to each other. I have often guessed by
people's faces what they were saying, though I could
not hear one word they said. The most material
knowledge of all—I mean the knowledge of the world
—is never to be acquired without great attention;
25 and I know many old people, who, though they have
lived long in the world, are but children still as to
the knowledge of it, from their levity and inattention.
Certain forms which all people comply with, and certain arts which all people aim at, hide in some degree
30 the truth and give a general exterior resemblance to

---

15 People can say, etc. An experienced diplomatist. Lord Chesterfield had
verified Talleyrand's saying that it is the province of language to conceal one's
thoughts.

almost everybody. Attention and sagacity must see
through that veil and discover the natural character.
You are at an age now to reflect, to observe and com-
pare characters, and to arm yourself against the
common arts,—at least of the world. If a man with 5
whom you are barely acquainted, and to whom you
have made no offers nor given any marks of friendship, makes you on a sudden strong professions of
his [friendship], receive them with civility, but do not
repay them with confidence; he certainly means to 10
deceive you, for one man does not fall in love with
another at sight. If a man uses strong protestations
or oaths to make you believe a thing which is of itself
so likely and probable that the bare saying of it would
be sufficient, depend upon it he lies, and is highly 15
interested in making you believe it; or else he would
not take so much pains.

In about five weeks I propose having the honor
of laying myself at your feet,—which I hope to find
grown longer than they were when I left them. 20
Adieu.

Letter X

THE FOLLY OF WHOLESALE DENUNCIATION

April 5, 1746.

DEAR BOY: Before it is very long, I am of opinion
that you will both think and speak more favorably
of women than you do now. You seem to think that 25
from Eve downward they have done a great deal
of mischief. As for that lady, I give her up to you:

---

[24] Young Stanhope had probably spoken slightingly of women, as many a silly
boy has since.

but since her time, history will inform you that men
have done much more mischief in the world than
women; and to say the truth, I would not advise you
to trust either more than is absolutely necessary. But
5 this I will advise you to, which is, never to attack
whole bodies of any kind; for besides that all general
rules have their exceptions, you unnecessarily make
yourself a great number of enemies by attacking a
corps collectively. Among women, as among men,
10 there are good as well as bad; and it may be full as
many or more good than among men. This rule
holds as to lawyers, soldiers, parsons, courtiers, citizens, etc. They are all men, subject to the same passions and sentiments, differing only in the manner,
15 according to their several educations; and it would
be as imprudent as unjust to attack any of them by
the lump. Individuals forgive sometimes; but bodies
and societies never do. Many young people think
it very genteel and witty to abuse the clergy; in which
20 they are extremely mistaken, since in my opinion parsons are very like men, and neither the better nor
the worse for wearing a black gown. All general
reflections upon nations and societies are the trite,
threadbare jokes of those who set up for wit without
25 having any, and so have recourse to commonplace.
Judge of individuals from your own knowledge of
them, and not from their sex, profession, or
denomination.

.   .   .   .

Letter XI

THE INTELLIGENT TRAVELER

BATH, Sept. 29, O. S. 1746.

DEAR BOY: I received by the last mail your letter of the 23 N. S. from Heidelberg, and am very well pleased to find that you inform yourself of the particulars of the several places you go through. You 5 do mighty right to see the curiosities in those several places, such as the Golden Bull at Frankfort, the Tun at Heidelberg, etc. Other travelers see and talk of them; it is very proper to see them, too, but remember that seeing is the least material object of travel- 10 ing,—hearing and knowing are the essential points. Therefore pray let your inquiries be chiefly directed to the knowledge of the constitution and particular customs of the places where you either reside at or pass through, whom they belong to, by what right 15 and tenure, and since when; in whom the supreme authority is lodged, and by what magistrates, and in what manner, the civil and criminal justice is administered. It is likewise necessary to get as much acquaintance as you can, in order to observe the 20 characters and manners of the people; for though human nature is in truth the same through the whole human species, yet it is so differently modified and varied by education, habit, and different customs, that

---

7 **Golden Bull.** A decree of the Emperor Charles IV., confirming the right of electing a German emperor in three spiritual and four temporal electors. A gold seal was affixed to the original document.

7 **Tun.** A large cask said to be 24 feet in diameter and 30 feet deep, containing 49,000 gallons.

one should, upon a slight and superficial observation, almost think it different.

As I have never been in Switzerland myself, I must desire you to inform me, now and then, of the con-
5 stitution of that country. As, for instance, do the Thirteen Cantons jointly and collectively form one government where the supreme authority is lodged, or is each canton sovereign in itself, and under no tie or constitutional obligation of acting in common
10 concert with the other cantons? Can any one canton make war or form an alliance with a foreign power without the consent of the other twelve or at least a majority of them? Can one canton declare war against another? If every canton is sovereign and
15 independent in itself, in whom is the supreme power of that canton lodged? Is it in one man, or in a certain number of men? If in one man, what is he called? If in a number, what are they called,— Senate, Council, or what? I do not suppose that you
20 can yet know these things yourself; but a very little inquiry of those who do will enable you to answer me these few questions in your next. You see, I am sure, the necessity of knowing these things thoroughly, and consequently the necessity of con-
25 versing much with the people of the country, who alone can inform you rightly; whereas, most of the English who travel converse only with each other, and consequently know no more when they return to England than they did when they left it. This pro-

---

° **Thirteen Cantons** at that time: twenty two since 1815. A study of Swiss political institutions, such as is here suggested by Lord Chesterfield. should have great interest for American youth. An English writer remarks, " Swiss history is *a study in federalism.*"

ceeds from a *mauvaise honte* which makes them
ashamed of going into company; and frequently, too,
from the want of the necessary language (French) to
enable them to bear their part in it. As for the
mauvaise honte, I hope you are above it. Your figure 5
is like other people's; I suppose you will care that
your dress shall be so, too, and to avoid any singularity. What, then, should you be ashamed of, and
why not go into a mixed company with as much ease
and as little concern as you would go into your own 10
room? Vice and ignorance are the only things I
know which one ought to be ashamed of; keep but
clear of them and you may go anywhere without fear
or concern. I have known some people who, from
feeling the pain and inconveniences of this *mauvaise* 15
honte, have rushed into the other extreme and turned
impudent, as cowards sometimes grow desperate from
the excess of danger; but this, too, is carefully to be
avoided, there being nothing more generally shocking than impudence. The medium between these 20
two extremes marks out the well-bred man; he feels
himself firm and easy in all companies; is modest
without being bashful, and steady without being
impudent; if he is a stranger, he observes with care
the manners and ways of the people most esteemed 25
at that place, and conforms to them with complaisance. Instead of finding fault with the customs of
that place and telling the people that the English
ones are a thousand times better,—as my countrymen are very apt to do,—he commends their table, 30
their dress, their houses, and their manners a little
more, it may be, than he really thinks they deserve.
But this degree of complaisance is neither criminal

nor abject, and is but a small price to pay for the good-will and affection of the people you converse with.   As the generality of people are weak enough to be pleased with these little things, those who refuse 5 to please them so cheaply are, in my mind, weaker than they.

·   ·   ·   ·   ·   ·   ·

Letter XII

THE KNOWLEDGE OF BOOKS AND OF MEN

BATH, Oct. 4th, O. S. 1746.

DEAR BOY: . . . I have often of late, reflected what an unhappy man I must now have been, if 10 I had not acquired in my youth some fund and taste of learning. What could I have done with myself, at this age, without them?   I must, as many ignorant people do, have destroyed my health and faculties by sotting away the evenings; or, by 15 wasting them frivolously in the tattle of women's company, must have exposed myself to the ridicule and contempt of those very women; or, lastly, I must have hanged myself, as a man once did, for weariness of putting on and pulling off his shoes and 20 stockings every day.   My books, and only my books, are now left me; and I daily find what Cicero says of learning to be true: "*Hæc studia* (says he)

Weaker than they.   No one should be deceived by this casuistry, which his lordship has himself condemned in Letter XXII.   The sacrifice of truth is never made "cheaply."

²² Hæc studia . . . . rusticantur.   A famous passage from Cicero: "Learning is the food of youth, the delight of old age : it is an ornament in prosperity, a refuge and a solace in adversity : it is a delight at home, and no impedi-

*adolescentiam alunt, senectutem oblectant, secundas res
ornant, adversis perfugium ac solatium præbent, delectant
domi, non impediunt foris, pernoctant nobiscum, pere-
grinantur, rusticantur."*

I do not mean, by this, to exclude conversation out 5
of the pleasures of an advanced age; on the contrary,
it is a very great and a very rational pleasure, at all
ages; but the conversation of the ignorant is no conversation, and gives even them no pleasure: they tire
of their own sterility, and have not matter enough 10
to furnish them with words to keep up a conversation.

Let me, therefore, most earnestly recommend to
you to hoard up, while you can, a great stock of
knowledge; for though, during the dissipation of your
youth, you may not have occasion to spend much of 15
it, yet you may depend upon it that a time will come,
when you will want it to maintain you. Public
granaries are filled in plentiful years; not that it is
known that the next, or the second, or the third year
will prove a scarce one, but because it is known that 20
sooner or later such a year will come, in which the
grain will be wanted.

I will say no more to you upon this subject; you
have Mr. Harte with you to enforce it; you have
Reason to assent to the truth of it; so that, in short, 25
" you have Moses and the Prophets; if you will not
believe them, neither will you believe, though one
rose from the dead."—Do not imagine that the knowledge, which I so much recommend to you, is confined

---

ment abroad : it stays with us during the night, in our wanderings, in our country
homes."

24 Mr. Harte. The boy's tutor.

26 " You have Moses," etc. St. Luke, xvi. 31.

to books, pleasing, useful, and necessary as that knowledge is: but I comprehend in it the great knowledge of the world, still more necessary than that of books.   In truth, they assist one another reciprocally; 5 and no man will have either perfectly. who has not both.   The knowledge of the world is only to be acquired in the world, and not in a closet.   Books alone will never teach it you; but they will suggest many things to your observation, which might other- 10 wise escape you; and your own observations upon mankind, when compared with those which you will find in books, will help you to fix the true point.

To know mankind well requires full as much attention and application as to know books, and, it may 15 be, more sagacity and discernment.   I am, at this time, acquainted with many elderly people, who have all passed their whole lives in the great world, but with such levity and inattention, that they know no more of it now than they did at fifteen.   Do not flatter 20 yourself, therefore, with the thoughts that you can acquire this knowledge in the frivolous chit-chat of idle companies: no, you must go much deeper than that.   You must look into people, as well as at them. Almost all people are born with all the passions, to 25 a certain degree; but almost every man has a prevailing one, to which the others are subordinate.   Search everyone for that ruling passion; pry into the recesses of his heart, and observe the different workings of the same passion in different people.   And, when you 30 have found out the prevailing passion of any man, remember never to trust him, where that passion is concerned.   Work upon him by it, if you please, but be upon your guard yourself against it, whatever professions he may make you.

Adieu.

CHESTERFIELD.

Letter XIII

THOUGHTFULNESS

BATH, October the 9th, O. S. 1746. 5

DEAR BOY: Your distresses in your journey from Heidelberg to Schaffhausen, your lying upon straw, your black bread, and your broken *Berline*, are proper seasonings for the greater fatigues and distresses, which you must expect in the course of your travels; 10 and, if one had a mind to moralize, one might call them samples of the accidents, rubs, and difficulties, which every man meets with in his journey through life. In this journey, the understanding is the *voiture* that must carry you through; and in proportion as 15 that is stronger or weaker, more or less in repair, your journey will be better or worse; though, at best, you will now and then find some bad roads, and some bad inns. Take care, therefore, to keep that necessary *voiture* in perfect good repair; examine, improve, 20 and strengthen it every day: it is in the power and ought to be the care, of every man to do it; he that neglects it deserves to feel, and certainly will feel, the fatal effects of that negligence.

A propos of negligence; I must say something to 25 you upon that subject. You know I have often told

---

8 **Berline.** A traveling carriage.
14 **Voiture.** Carriage.

you that my affection for you was not a weak, woman-
ish one; and, far from blinding me, it makes me but
more quick-sighted as to your faults: those it is not
only my right, but my duty to tell you of, and it is
5 your duty and your interest to correct them.   In the
strict scrutiny which I have made into you, I have
(thank God) hitherto not discovered any vice of the
heart, or any peculiar weakness of the head: but I
have discovered laziness, inattention, and indiffer-
10 ence; faults which are only pardonable in old men,
who, in the decline of life, when health and spirits
fail, have a kind of claim to that sort of tranquillity.
But a young man should be ambitious to shine and
excel; alert, active, and indefatigable in the means of
15 doing it; and, like Cæsar, *Nil actum reputans, si quid
superesset agendum.*   You seem to want that *vivida
vis animi* which spurs and excites most young men
to please, to shine, to excel.   Without the desire and
the pains necessary to be considerable, depend upon
20 it you never can be so; as, without the desire and
attention necessary to please, you never can please.
Nullum numen abest, si sit prudentia, is unquestionably
true with regard to everything except poetry; and I
am very sure that any man of common understanding
25 may, by proper culture, care, attention, and labor,
make himself whatever he pleases except a good poet.
Your destination is the great and busy world; your
immediate object is the affairs, the interests, and the

---

¹⁵ Nil actum . . . . agendum.   "Think nothing done as long as anything
remains undone "

¹⁶ Vivida vis animi.   Vigorous force of mind

²² Nullum numen abest, si sit prudentia.   " Every power is present when
application is present."   See note to line 12, page 157.

history, the constitutions, the customs, and the
manners of the several parts of Europe. In this any
man of common sense may, by common application,
be sure to excel. Ancient and Modern History are,
by attention, easily attainable. Geography and Chro- 5
nology the same; none of them requiring any uncommon share of genius or invention. Speaking and
writing clearly, correctly, and with ease and grace,
are certainly to be acquired by reading the best
authors with care, and by attention to the best living 10
models. These are the qualifications more particularly necessary for you in your department, which
you may be possessed of if you please, and which,
I tell you fairly, I shall be very angry at you if you
are not; because, as you have the means in your 15
hands, it will be your own fault only.

If care and application are necessary to the acquiring of those qualifications, without which you can
never be considerable nor make a figure in the world,
they are not less necessary with regard to the lesser 20
accomplishments, which are requisite to make you
agreeable and pleasing in society. In truth, whatever is worth doing at all is worth doing well, and
nothing can be done well without attention: I therefore carry the necessity of attention down to the low- 25
est things, even to dancing and dress. Custom has
made dancing sometimes necessary for a young man;
therefore mind it while you learn it, that you may
learn to do it well, and not be ridiculous, though in
a ridiculous act. Dress is of the same nature; you 30

---

¹² **Your department.** Lord Chesterfield intended his son for a public
career.

must dress, therefore attend to it; not in order to
rival or to excel a fop in it, but in order to avoid
singularity, and consequently ridicule. Take great
care always to be dressed like the reasonable people
5 of your own age, in the place where you are, whose
dress is never spoken of one way or another, as either
too negligent or too much studied.

What is commonly called an absent man, is commonly either a very weak or a very affected man; but
10 be he which he will, he is, I am sure, a very disagreeable man in company. He fails in all the
common offices of civility; he seems not to know
those people to-day with whom yesterday he appeared
to live in intimacy. He takes no part in the general
15 conversation; but, on the contrary, breaks into it
from time to time with some start of his own, as if
he waked from a dream. This (as I said before) is
a sure indication either of a mind so weak that it is
not able to bear above one object at a time; or so
20 affected, that it would be supposed to be wholly
engrossed by, and directed to, some very great and
important objects. Sir Isaac Newton, Mr. Locke,
and (it may be) five or six more, since the creation of
the world, may have had a right to absence, from
25 that intense thought which the things they were
investigating required. But if a young man, and a
man of the world, who has no such avocations to
plead, will claim and exercise that right of absence
in company, his pretended right should, in my mind,
30 be turned into an involuntary absence, by his perpetual exclusion out of company. However frivolous

---

[22] **Newton ; Locke.** Both noted for absent-mindedness.

a company may be, still, while you are among them,
do not show them, by your inattention, that you think
them so; but rather take their tone, and conform in
some degree to their weakness, instead of manifesting
your contempt for them. There is nothing that 5
people bear more impatiently, or forgive less, than
contempt: and an injury is much sooner forgotten
than an insult.

My long and frequent letters which I send you, in
great doubt of their success, put me in mind of cer- 10
tain papers which you have very lately, and I formerly, sent up to kites, along the string, which we
called messengers; some of them the wind used to
blow away, others were torn by the string, and but
few of them got up and stuck to the kite. But I will 15
content myself now, as I did then, if some of my
present messengers do but stick to you. Adieu.

Letter XIV

TRUE PLEASURE NOT VICE

LONDON, March the 27th, O. S. 1747.

DEAR BOY: Pleasure is the rock which most young
people split upon; they launch out with crowded sails 20
in quest of it, but without a compass to direct their
course, or reason sufficient to steer the vessel; for
want of which, pain and shame, instead of Pleasure,
are the returns of their voyage. Do not think that
I mean to snarl at Pleasure, like a Stoic, or to preach 25
against it, like a Parson; no, I mean to point it out,
and recommend it to you, like an Epicurean: I wish

you a great deal, and my only view is to hinder you
from mistaking it.

The character which most young men first aim at
is, that of a Man of Pleasure; but they generally take
5 it upon trust; and instead of consulting their own
taste and inclinations, they blindly adopt whatever
those with whom they chiefly converse are pleased to
call by the name of Pleasure; and a *Man of Pleasure*,
in the vulgar acceptation of that phrase, means only
10 a beastly drunkard, an abandoned rake, and a profligate swearer and curser.   As it may be of use to you,
I am not unwilling, though at the same time ashamed,
to own that the vices of my youth proceeded much
more from my silly resolution of being what I heard
15 called a Man of Pleasure, than from my own inclinations.   I always naturally hated drinking; and yet
I have often drunk, with disgust at the time, attended
by great sickness the next day, only because I then
considered drinking as a necessary qualification for a
20 fine gentleman and a Man of Pleasure.

The same as to gaming.   I did not want money,
and consequently had no occasion to play for it; but
I thought Play another necessary ingredient in the
composition of a Man of Pleasure, and accordingly
25 I plunged into it without desire, at first; sacrificed a

---

[21] **Gaming.**   Lord Chesterfield's detestation of gambling is seen in the following
extract from his will :

" In case my said godson, Philip Stanhope, [his heir] shall, at any time hereafter, keep, or be concerned in keeping of any race horses, or pack of hounds: or
reside one night at Newmarket, that infamous seminary of iniquity and ill-manners,
during the course of the races there : or shall resort to the said races : or shall lose
in any one day, at any game or bet whatsoever, the sum of £500 : then, in any of
the cases aforesaid, it is my express will that he, my said godson shall forfeit and
pay, out of my estate, the sum of £5000, to and for the use of the Dean and Chap-
·er of Westminster."

thousand real pleasures to it; and made myself solidly uneasy by it, for thirty of the best years of my life.

I was even absurd enough, for a little while, to swear, by way of adorning and completing the shining character which I affected; but this folly I soon laid aside upon finding both the guilt and the indecency of it.

Thus seduced by fashion, and blindly adopting nominal pleasures, I lost real ones; and my fortune impaired, and my constitution shattered, are, I must confess, the just punishment of my errors.

Take warning, then, by them; choose your pleasures for yourself, and do not let them be imposed upon you. Follow nature, and not fashion: weigh the present enjoyment of your pleasures against the necessary consequences of them, and then let your own common sense determine your choice.

Letter XV

ATTIC SALT

London, April the 3d, O. S. 1747.

Dear Boy: If I am rightly informed, I am now writing to a fine Gentleman, in a scarlet coat laced with gold, a brocade waistcoat, and all other suitable ornaments. The natural partiality of every author for his own works, makes me very glad to hear that Mr. Harte has thought this last edition of mine worth so fine a binding; and as he has bound it in red and gilt it upon the back, I hope he will take care that it shall be *lettered* too. A showish binding attracts the eyes, and engages the attention of everybody; but

with this difference, that women, and men who are like women, mind the binding more than the book; whereas men of sense and learning immediately examine the inside; and if they find that it does not
5 answer the finery on the outside, they throw it by with the greater indignation and contempt. I hope that when this edition of my works shall be opened and read, the best judges will find connection, consistency, solidity, and spirit in it. Mr. Harte may
10 *recensere* and *emendare* as much as he pleases, but it will be to little purpose if you do not coöperate with him. The work will be imperfect.

I like your account of the salt works; which shows that you gave some attention while you were seeing
15 them. But, notwithstanding that, by your account, the Swiss salt is (I dare say) very good, yet I am apt to suspect that it falls a little short of the true Attic salt, in which there was a peculiar quickness and delicacy. That same Attic salt seasoned almost all
20 Greece, except Bœotia; and a great deal of it was exported afterward to Rome, where it was counterfeited by a composition called Urbanity, which in some time was brought to very near the perfection of the original Attic salt. The more you are powdered
25 with these two kinds of salt, the better you will keep, and the more you will be relished.

Adieu! My compliments to Mr. Harte and Mr. Eliot.

---

10 **Recensere,** Revise : **Emendare,** Correct. Used of authors' revisions of their works.

17 **Attic salt.** A delicate wit, supposed to be peculiar to the Athenians.

20 **Bœotia.** Attic writers characterized the Bœotians as boorish.

Letter XVI

ONE THING AT A TIME

LONDON, April the 14th, O. S. 1747.

DEAR BOY: If you feel half the pleasure from the consciousness of doing well, that I do from the informations I have lately received in your favor from Mr. Harte, I shall have little occasion to exhort or ad-5 monish you any more, to do what your own satisfaction and self-love will sufficiently prompt you to. Mr. Harte tells me that you attend, that you apply to your studies; and that, beginning to understand, you begin to taste them. This pleasure will increase and 10 keep pace with your attention, so that the balance will be greatly to your advantage. You may remember, that I have always earnestly recommended to you, to do what you are about, be that what it will; and to do nothing else at the same time. Do not 15 imagine that I mean by this, that you should attend to, and plod at, your book all day long; far from it: I mean that you should have your pleasures too; and that you should attend to them, for the time, as much as to your studies; and if you do not attend equally 20 to both, you will neither have improvement nor satisfaction from either. A man is fit for neither business nor pleasure who either cannot, or does not, command and direct his attention to the present object, and in some degree banish, for that time, all other 25 objects from his thoughts. If at a ball, a supper, or a party of pleasure, a man were to be solving, in his own mind, a problem in Euclid, he would be a very

bad companion, and make a very poor figure in that company; or if, in studying a problem in his closet, he were to think of a minuet, I am apt to believe that he would make a very poor mathematician. There
5 is time enough for everything, in the course of the day, if you do but one thing at once; but there is not time enough in the year, if you will do two things at a time. The Pensionary de Witt, who was torn to pieces in the year 1672, did the whole business of the
10 Republic, and yet had time left to go to assemblies in the evening, and sup in company. Being asked how he could possibly find time to go through so much business, and yet amuse himself in the evenings as he did? he answered, There was nothing so easy;
15 for that it was only doing one thing at a time, and never putting off anything till to-morrow that could be done to-day. This steady and undissipated attention to one object is a sure mark of a superior genius; as hurry, bustle, and agitation, are the never-failing
20 symptoms of a weak and frivolous mind. When you read Horace, attend to the justness of his thoughts, the happiness of his diction, and the beauty of his poetry; and do not think of Puffendorf *de Homine et Cive:* and when you are reading Puffendorf, do not think of Madame de St. Germain; nor of Puffendorf, when you are talking to Madame de St. Germain.

---

⁸ **Pensionary de Witt.** (1625–1672.) John de Witt, Grand Pensionary of Holland, one of the greatest of Holland's great men. His death by an infuriated mob was due partly to a misunderstanding of his official acts, partly to the enmity of the Orange family.

²² **Puffendorf,** (or Pufendorf), (1632–1694,) a noted Saxon writer on jurisprudence, professor, successively, at Leyden, Heidelberg, and Lund. His work *De Officiis Hominis et Civis,* " On the Duty of the Man and of the Citizen," is an abridgment of a larger work.

Letter XVII

FRIENDSHIPS: COMPANY

LONDON, October the 9th, O. S. 1747.

DEAR BOY: People of your age have commonly an unguarded frankness about them, which makes them the easy prey and bubbles of the artful and the experienced: they look upon every knave, or fool, 5 who tells them that he is their friend, to be really so; and pay that profession of simulated friendship with an indiscreet and unbounded confidence, always to their loss, often to their ruin. Beware, therefore, now that you are coming into the world, of these 10 proffered friendships. Receive them with great civility, but with great incredulity too; and pay them with compliments, but not with confidence. Do not let your vanity and self-love make you suppose that people become your friends at first sight, or even upon 15 a short acquaintance. Real friendship is a slow grower; and never thrives, unless ingrafted upon a stock of known and reciprocal merit. There is another kind of nominal friendship, among young people, which is warm for the time, but, by good luck, 20 of short duration. This friendship is hastily produced by their being accidentally thrown together, and pursuing the same course of riot and debauchery. A fine friendship, truly! and well cemented by drunkenness and lewdness. It should rather be 25 called a conspiracy against morals and good manners, and be punished as such by the civil Magistrate.

---

⁴ Bubbles. Dupes.

However, they have the impudence and the folly to
call this confederacy a friendship. They lend one
another money for bad purposes; they engage in
quarrels, offensive and defensive, for their accom-
5 plices; they tell one another all they know, and often
more too; when, of a sudden, some accident disperses
them, and they think no more of each other, unless it
be to betray and laugh at their imprudent confidence.
Remember to make a great difference between com-
10 panions and friends; for a very complaisant and
agreeable companion may, and often does, prove a
very improper and a very dangerous friend. People
will, in a great degree, and not without reason, form
their opinion of you upon that which they have of
15 your friends; and there is a Spanish proverb, which
says very justly, *Tell me whom you live with, and I will
tell you who you are*. One may fairly suppose that a
man who makes a knave or a fool his friend, has something very bad to do, or to conceal. But, at the same
20 time that you carefully decline the friendship of
knaves and fools, if it can be called friendship, there
is no occasion to make either of them your enemies,
wantonly and unprovoked; for they are numerous
bodies; and I would rather choose a secure neu-
25 trality, than alliance or war, with either of them. You
may be a declared enemy to their vices and follies,
without being marked out by them as a personal one.
Their enmity is the next dangerous thing to their
friendship. Have a real reserve with almost every-
30 body; and have a seeming reserve with almost
nobody; for it is very disagreeable to seem reserved,
and very dangerous not to be so. Few people find
the true medium; many are ridiculously mysterious

and reserved upon trifles; and many imprudently communicative of all they know.

The next thing to the choice of your friends is the choice of your company.   Endeavor, as much as you can, to keep company with people above you.   There 5 you rise, as much as you sink with people below you; for (as I have mentioned before) you are whatever the company you keep is.   Do not mistake, when I say company above you, and think that I mean with regard to their birth; that is the least consideration: 10 but I mean with regard to their merit, and the light in which the world considers them.

There are two sorts of good company; one which is called the *beau monde,* and consists of those people who have the lead in Courts, and in the gay part of 15 life; the other consists of those who are distinguished by some peculiar merit, or who excel in some particular and valuable art or science.   For my own part, I used to think myself in company as much above me, when I was with Mr. Addison and Mr. Pope, as if I 20 had been with all the princes in Europe.   What I mean by low company, which should by all means be avoided, is the company of those who, absolutely insignificant and contemptible in themselves, think they are honored by being in your company, and who 25 flatter every vice and every folly you have, in order to engage you to converse with them.   The pride of being the first of the company is but too common; but it is very silly, and very prejudicial.   Nothing in the world lets down a character more than that wrong 30 turn.

You may possibly ask me whether a man has it always in his power to get into the best company?

and how? I say, Yes, he has, by deserving it; provided he is but in circumstances which enable him to appear upon the footing of a gentleman. Merit and good breeding will make their way everywhere.
5 Knowledge will introduce him, and good breeding will endear him to the best companies; for, as I have often told you, politeness and good breeding are absolutely necessary to adorn any or all other good qualities or talents. Without them, no knowledge,
10 no perfection whatsoever, is seen in its best light. The Scholar, without good breeding, is a Pedant; the Philosopher, a Cynic; the Soldier, a Brute; and every man disagreeable.

I long to hear from my several correspondents at
15 Leipsig, of your arrival there, and what impression you make on them at first; for I have Arguses, with a hundred eyes each, who will watch you narrowly, and relate to me faithfully. My accounts will certainly be true; it depends upon you entirely of what
20 kind they shall be. Adieu.

Letter XVIII

THE USE AND VALUE OF TIME

London, December the 11th, O. S. 1747.
Dear Boy: There is nothing which I more wish that you should know, and which fewer people do know, than the true use and value of Time. It is in
25 everybody's mouth, but in few people's practice. Every fool, who slatterns away his whole time in

---

16 **Arguses.** In Greek mythology, Argus, the guardian of Io, had one hundred eyes.

nothings, utters, however, some trite commonplace sentence, of which there are millions, to prove at once the value and the fleetness of time. The sun-dials, likewise, all over Europe, have some ingenious inscription to that effect; so that nobody squanders 5 away their time without hearing and seeing daily how necessary it is to employ it well, and how irrecoverable it is if lost. But all these admonitions are useless, where there is not a fund of good sense and reason to suggest them, rather than receive them. 10 By the manner in which you now tell me that you employ your time, I flatter myself that you have that fund: that is the fund which will make you rich indeed. I do not, therefore, mean to give you a critical essay upon the use and abuse of time; I will only 15 give you some hints with regard to the use of one particular period of that long time which, I hope, you have before you; I mean the next two years. Remember, then, that whatever knowledge you do not solidly lay the foundation of before you are eighteen, 20 you will never be master of while you breathe. Knowledge is a comfortable and necessary retreat and shelter for us in an advanced age; and if we do not plant it while young, it will give us no shade when we grow old. I neither require nor expect from you 25 great application to books, after you are once thrown out into the great world. I know it is impossible; and it may even, in some cases, be improper: this, therefore, is your time, and your only time, for unwearied and uninterrupted application. If ·you should some- 30 times think it a little laborious, consider that labor is the unavoidable fatigue of a necessary journey. The more hours a day you travel, the sooner you will be

at your journey's end. The sooner you are qualified for your liberty, the sooner you shall have it; and your manumission will entirely depend upon the manner in which you employ the intermediate time.
5 I think I offer you a very good bargain, when I promise you, upon my word, that if you will do everything that I would have you do, till you are eighteen, I will do everything that you would have me do, ever afterward.

Letter XIX

BE THOROUGH

10 BATH, February the 16th, O. S. 1748.
DEAR BOY: The first use that I made of my liberty was to come hither, where I arrived yesterday. My health, though not fundamentally bad, yet for want of proper attention of late wanted some repairs, which 15 these waters never fail giving it. I shall drink them a month, and return to London, there to enjoy the comforts of social life, instead of groaning under the load of business. I have given the description of the life that I propose to lead for the future, in this 20 motto, which I have put up in the frieze of my library in my new house:

Nunc veterum libris, nunc somno, et inertibus horis
Ducere sollicitæ jucunda oblivia vitæ.

I must observe to you, upon this occasion, that the 25 uninterrupted satisfaction which I expect to find in that library, will be chiefly owing to my having em-

---

[21] **New house.** In London.
[22] **Nunc . . . . vitæ.** Horace, Satires, II. 6, 62. "In agreeable forgetfulness of the cares of life, I devote myself to ancient literature, to sleep, and to leisure."

ployed some part of my life well at your age. I wish
I had employed it better, and my satisfaction would
now be complete; but, however, I planted, while
young, that degree of knowledge which is now my
refuge and my shelter. Make your plantations still 5
more extensive, they will more than pay you for your
trouble. I do not regret the time that I passed in
pleasures; they were seasonable, they were the
pleasures of youth, and I enjoyed them while young.
If I had not, I should probably have overvalued them 10
now, as we are very apt to do what we do not know:
but, knowing them as I do, I know their real value,
and how much they are generally overrated. Nor do
I regret the time that I have passed in business, for
the same reason; those who see only the outside of it 15
imagine that it has hidden charms, which they pant
after; and nothing but acquaintance can undeceive
them. I, who have been behind the scenes, both of
pleasure and business, and have seen all the springs
and pullies of those decorations which astonish and 20
dazzle the audience, retire, not only without regret,
but with contentment and satisfaction. But what I
do and ever shall regret, is the time which, while
young, I lost in mere idleness and in doing nothing.
This is the common effect of the inconsideracy of 25
youth, against which I beg you will be most carefully
upon your guard. The value of moments, when cast
up, is immense, if well employed; if thrown away,
their loss is irrecoverable. Every moment may be
put to some use, and that with much more pleasure 30
than if unemployed. Do not imagine that, by the
employment of time, I mean an uninterrupted application to serious studies. No; pleasures are, at

proper times, both as necessary and as useful: they
fashion and form you for the world; they teach you
characters, and show you the human heart in its unguarded minutes. But, then, remember to make that
5 use of them. I have known many people, from laziness of mind, go through both pleasure and business
with equal inattention; neither enjoying the one, nor
doing the other; thinking themselves men of pleasure, because they were mingled with those who were;
10 and men of business, because they had business to do,
though they did not do it. Whatever you do, do
it to the purpose; do it thoroughly, not superficially.
Approfondissez; go to the bottom of things. Anything half done, or half known, is, in my mind, neither
15 done nor known at all. Nay worse, for it often mis-
leads. There is hardly any place, or any company,
where you may not gain knowledge if you please;
almost everybody knows some one thing, and is glad
to talk upon that one thing. Seek and you will find,
20 in this world as well as in the next. See everything,
inquire into everything; and you may excuse your
curiosity, and the questions you ask, which otherwise
might be thought impertinent, by your manner of asking them; for most things depend a great deal upon
25 the manner. As, for example, *I am afraid that I am
very troublesome with my questions; but nobody can
inform me so well as you;* or something of that kind.

. . . .

I have now but one anxiety left which is concern-
ing you. I would have you be, what I know nobody
30 is, perfect. As that is impossible, I would have you
as near perfection as possible. I know nobody in a

---

13 Approfondissez. Go to the bottom of things.

fairer way toward it than yourself if you please.
Never were so much pains taken for anybody's education as for yours; and never had anybody those
opportunities of knowledge and improvement which
you have had and still have.   I hope, I wish, I doubt, 5
and I fear alternately.   This only I am sure of, that
you will prove either the greatest pain or the greatest
pleasure of   Yours.

Letter XX

THE MODESTY OF TRUE LEARNING

BATH, February the 22d, O. S. 1748.
DEAR BOY: Every excellency, and every virtue, 10
has its kindred vice or weakness; and if carried beyond certain bounds, sinks into the one or the other.
Generosity often runs into Profusion, Economy into
Avarice, Courage into Rashness, Caution into
Timidity, and so on:—insomuch that, I believe, there 15
is more judgment required for the proper conduct of
our virtues, than for avoiding their opposite vices.
Vice, in its true light, is so deformed, that it shocks
us at first sight; and would hardly ever seduce us. if
it did not at first wear the mask of some Virtue.   But 20
Virtue is in itself so beautiful, that it charms us at
first sight; engages us more and more, upon further
acquaintance; and, as with other Beauties, we think
excess impossible: it is here that judgment is neces-

---

¹⁴ Vice.   " Vice is a monster of so frightful mien,
                       As, to be hated, needs but to be seen ;
                       Yet seen too oft, familiar with her face,
                       We first endure,—then pity, then embrace."
                                                    —Pope's *Essay on Man*, II, 217.

sary to moderate and direct the effects of an excellent
cause.   I shall apply this reasoning, at present, not
to any particular virtue, but to an excellency, which
for want of judgment is often the cause of ridiculous
5 and blamable effects; I mean, great Learning, which,
if not accompanied with sound judgment, frequently
carries us into Error, Pride, and Pedantry.   As I
hope you will possess that excellency in its utmost
extent, and yet without its too common failings, the
10 hints which my experience can suggest may probably not be useless to you.

Some learned men, proud of their knowledge, only
speak to decide, and give judgment without appeal.
The consequence of which is, that mankind, provoked
15 by the insult, and injured by the oppression, revolt;
and in order to shake off the tyranny, even call the
lawful authority in question.   The more you know,
the modester you should be: and (by the by) that
modesty is the surest way of gratifying your vanity.
20 Even where you are sure, seem rather doubtful:
represent, but do not pronounce; and if you would
convince others, seem open to conviction yourself.

Others, to show their learning, or often from the
prejudices of a school education, where they hear of
25 nothing else, are always talking of the Ancients as
something more than men, and of the Moderns as
something less.   They are never without a Classic
or two in their pockets; they stick to the old good
sense; they read none of the modern trash; and will
30 show you plainly that no improvement has been made
in any one art or science these last seventeen hundred
years.   I would by no means have you disown your
acquaintance with the Ancients; but still less would I

have you brag of an exclusive intimacy with them.
Speak of the Moderns without contempt, and of the
Ancients without idolatry; judge them all by their
merits, but not by their ages; and if you happen to
have an Elzevir classic in your pocket, neither show 5
it nor mention it.

· Some great Scholars most absurdly draw all their
maxims, both for public and private life, from what
they call Parallel Cases in the ancient authors; without considering, that, in the first place, there never 10
were, since the creation of the world, two cases
exactly parallel: and, in the next place, that there
never was a case stated, or even known, by any Historian, with every one of its circumstances; which,
however, ought to be known, in order to be reasoned 15
from. Reason upon the case itself and the several
circumstances that attend it, and act accordingly: but
not from the authority of ancient Poets or Historians.
Take into your consideration, if you please, cases
seemingly analogous; but take them as helps only, 20
not as guides. We are really so prejudiced by our
educations, that, as the Ancients deified their Heroes,
we deify their Madmen: of which, with all due regard
to antiquity, I take Leonidas and Curtius to have been
two distinguished ones. And yet a stolid Pedant 25
would, in a speech in Parliament, relative to a tax of
twopence in the pound, upon some commodity or
other, quote those two heroes, as examples of what

---

³ **Elzevir classic.** The Elzevirs, publishers, of Amsterdam and Leyden,
issued editions of the classics and of the New Testament, celebrated for the beauty
of their typography. (1592–1681.)

²⁴ **Leonidas and Curtius.** Leonidas sacrificed his life at Thermopylæ in
battle with the Persians, in obedience to the laws of his native Sparta. Tradition
says that Curtius leaped into a chasm in order to save Rome.

we ought to do and suffer for our country. I have
known these absurdities carried so far, by people of
injudicious learning, that I should not be surprised,
if some of them were to propose, while we are at war
5 with the Gauls, that a number of geese should be
kept in the Tower, upon account of the infinite advantage which Rome received, *in a parallel case*, from a
certain number of geese in the Capitol. This way
of reasoning, and this way of speaking, will always
10 form a poor politician, and a puerile declaimer.

There is another species of learned men, who,
though less dogmatical and supercilious, are not less
impertinent. These are the communicative and shining Pedants, who adorn their conversation, even with
15 women, by happy quotations of Greek and Latin, and
who have contracted such a familiarity with the Greek
and Roman authors, that they call them by certain
names or epithets denoting intimacy. As *old* Homer;
that *sly rogue* Horace; *Maro*, instead of Virgil; and
20 *Naso*, instead of Ovid. These are often imitated by
coxcombs who have no learning at all, but who have
got some names and some scraps of ancient authors
by heart, which they improperly and impertinently
retail in all companies, in hopes of passing for
25 scholars. If, therefore, you would avoid the accusa-
tion of pedantry, on one hand, or the suspicion of
ignorance, on the other, abstain from learned ostentation. Speak the language of the company that you

---

⁵ **Gauls,** *i. e.*, the French. While the ancient Gauls were besieging the capitol
of Rome, their night attack was made known to the sleeping garrison by the cack-
ling of geese.

¹⁹ **Maro.** Publius Vergilius Maro, Virgil.

²⁰ **Naso.** Publius Ovidius Naso, Ovid.

are in; speak it purely, and unlarded with any other. Never seem wiser, nor more learned, than the people you are with. Wear your learning, like your watch, in a private pocket; and do not pull it out, and strike it, merely to show that you have one. If you are 5 asked what o'clock it is, tell it; but do not proclaim it hourly and unasked, like the watchman.

Upon the whole, remember that learning (I mean Greek and Roman learning) is a most useful and necessary ornament, which it is sl ameful not to be 10 master of; but at the same time most carefully avoid those errors and abuses which I have mentioned, and which too often attend it. Remember, too, that great modern knowledge is still more necessary than ancient; and that you had better know perfectly the 15 present than the old state of Europe; though I would have you well acquainted with both.

Letter XXI

THE LAZY MIND: THE FRIVOLOUS MIND

LONDON, July the 26th, O. S. 1748.
DEAR BOY: There are two sorts of understandings; one of which hinders a man from ever being con- 20 siderable, and the other commonly makes him ridiculous; I mean the lazy mind, and the trifling, frivolous mind. Yours, I hope, is neither. The lazy mind will not take the trouble of going to the bottom of anything, but, discouraged by the first difficulties 25 (and everything worth knowing or having is attended with some), stops short, contents itself with easy, and consequently superficial, knowledge, and prefers a

great degree of ignorance to a small degree of trouble. These people either think or represent most things as impossible, whereas few things are so to industry and activity. But difficulties seem to them
5 impossibilities, or at least they pretend to think them so, by way of excuse for their laziness. An hour's attention to the same object is too laborious for them; they take everything in the light in which it first presents itself, never consider it in all its different views,
10 and, in short, never think it thorough. The consequence of this is, that when they come to speak upon these subjects before people who have considered them with attention, they only discover their own ignorance and laziness, and lay themselves open to
15 answers that put them in confusion. Do not, then, be discouraged by the first difficulties, but *contra audentior ito;* and resolve to go to the bottom of all those things which every gentleman ought to know well. Those arts or sciences which are peculiar to
20 certain professions need not be deeply known by those who are not intended for those professions. As, for instance, fortification and navigation; of both which, a superficial and general knowledge, such as the common course of conversation,
25 with a very little inquiry on your part, will give you, is sufficient. Though, by the way, a little more knowledge of fortification may be of some use to you; as the events of war, in sieges, make many of the terms of that science occur frequently in common
30 conversations; and one would be sorry to say, like the

---

[16] **Contra audentior ito.** " *Tu ne cede malis sed contra audentior ito.*" Æneid, VI. 95. "Yet do not yield to your ills, but advance ever bolder against them." Howland's translation.

Marquis de Mascarille, in Molière's *Précieuses Ridi-cules*, when he hears of *une demi Lune; Ma foi c'étoit bien une Lune toute entière*. But those things which every gentleman, independently of profession, should know, he ought to know well, and dive into all the depths of them. Such are languages, history, and geography ancient and modern; philosophy, rational logic, rhetoric; and, for you particularly, the constitution, and the civil and military state, of every country in Europe. This, I confess, is a pretty large circle of knowledge, attended with some difficulties, and requiring some trouble; which, however, an active and industrious mind will overcome, and be amply repaid. The trifling and frivolous mind is always busied, but to little purpose; it takes little objects for great ones, and throws away upon trifles that time and attention which only important things deserve. Knick-knacks, butterflies, shells, insects, etc., are the objects of their most serious researches. They contemplate the dress, not the characters, of the company they keep. They attend more to the decorations of a Play, than to the sense of it; and to the ceremonies of a Court, more than to its politics. Such an employment of time is an absolute loss of it. You have now, at most, three years to employ either well or ill; for as I have often told you, you will be all your life what you shall be three years hence. For God's sake, then, reflect: Will you throw away this time, either in laziness, or in trifles? Or will you not rather employ every moment of it in a manner that

¹ Précieuses Ridicules. A comedy by Molière.
² Une demi Lune. A half moon : in fortification, an outwork.
³ Ma foi . . . . entière. "Faith, surely, it is a full moon."

must so soon reward you, with so much pleasure, figure, and character? I cannot, I will not, doubt of your choice. Read only useful books; and never quit a subject till you are thoroughly master of it, 5 but read and inquire on till then. When you are in company, bring the conversation to some useful subject, but *à portée* of that company. Points of history, matters of literature, the customs of particular countries, the several Orders of Knighthood, as Teutonic, 10 Maltese, etc., are surely better subjects of conversation than the weather, dress, or fiddle-faddle stories, that carry no information along with them. The characters of Kings, and great Men, are only to be learned in conversation; for they are never fairly 15 written during their lives. This, therefore, is an entertaining and instructive subject of conversation, and will likewise give you an opportunity of observing how very differently characters are given, from the different passions and views of those who give 20 them. Never be ashamed nor afraid of asking questions; for if they lead to information, and if you accompany them with some excuse, you will never be reckoned an impertinent or rude questioner. All those things, in the common course of life, depend 25 entirely upon the manner; and in that respect the vulgar saying is true, That one man may better steal a horse, than another look over the hedge. There

---

⁸ **Read only useful books.** In another letter his lordship writes: " But throw away none of your time upon those trivial futile books published by idle or necessitous authors for the amusement of idle and ignorant readers : such books swarm and buzz about me every day ; flap them away ; they have no sting ; *certum pete finem ;* have some one object for your leisure moments, and pursue that object invariably till you have obtained it."

⁷ **À portée.** Within the comprehension of.

are few things that may not be said, in some manner
or other; either in a seeming confidence, or a genteel
irony, or introduced with wit: and one great part of
the knowledge of the world consists in knowing when
and where to make use of these different manners. 5
The graces of the person, the countenance, and the
way of speaking, contribute so much to this, that I
am convinced the very same thing said by a genteel
person, in an engaging way, and *gracefully* and distinctly spoken, would please; which would shock, if 10
muttered out by an awkward figure, with a sullen,
serious countenance. The Poets always represent
Venus as attended by the three Graces, to intimate
that even Beauty will not do without. I think they
should have given Minerva three also; for without 15
them, I am sure, learning is very unattractive.
Invoke them, then, *distinctly*, to accompany all your
words and motions. Adieu.

Letter XXII

AGAINST CASUISTRY

LONDON, Sept. 27, O. S. 1748.

Pray let no quibbles of lawyers, no refinement of 20
casuists, break into the plain notions of right and
wrong which every man's right reason and plain

---

¹² **Venus.** The goddess of love and beauty.

¹³ **Graces.** The name usually given to the Greek goddesses *Charites—Aglaia*, *Euphrosyne*, and *Thalia*, the personifications of beauty, grace, and cheerfulness, in nature and in morals.

¹⁵ **Minerva.** The goddess of wisdom: Athena.

common sense suggest to him.   To do as you would
be done by is the plain, sure, and undisputed rule of
morality and justice.   Stick to that; and be convinced
that whatever breaks into it in any degree, however
5 speciously it may be termed, and however puzzling
it may be to answer it, is notwithstanding false in
itself, unjust, and criminal.   I do not know a crime
in the world which is not by casuists allowed in some
or many cases not to be criminal.   The principles
10 first laid down by them are often specious, the reasonings plausible, but the conclusion always a lie; for
it is contrary to that evident and undeniable rule of
justice which I have mentioned above, of not doing
to anyone what you would not have him do to you.
15 But, however, these refined pieces of casuistry and
sophistry being very convenient and welcome to
people's passions and appetites, they gladly accept
the indulgence without desiring to detect the fallacy
of the reasoning: and indeed many, I might say most
20 people, are not able to do it,—which makes the publication of such quibblings and refinements the more
pernicious.   I am no skillful casuist nor subtle dis-
putant; and yet I would undertake to justify and
qualify the profession of a highwayman, step by step,
25 and so plausibly as to make many ignorant people
embrace the profession as an innocent if not even a
laudable one, and to puzzle people of some degree
of knowledge to answer me point by point.   I have
seen a book, entitled " Quidlibet ex Quolibet," or
30 the art of making anything out of anything; which is
not so difficult as it would seem, if one once quits

---

29 Quidlibet ex quolibet.   " Whatever you please from whatever you please."
That is: Any conclusion may be derived from any premises.

certain plain truths, obvious in gross to every understanding, in order to run after the ingenious refinements of warm imaginations and speculative reasonings. Doctor Berkeley, Bishop of Cloyne, a very worthy, ingenious, and learned man, has written a 5 book to prove that there is no such thing as matter, and that nothing exists but in idea; that you and I only fancy ourselves eating, drinking, and sleeping, you at Leipsig, and I at London; that we think we have flesh and blood, legs, arms, etc., but that we 10 are only spirit. His arguments are, strictly speaking, unanswerable; but yet I am so far from being convinced by them that I am determined to go on to eat and drink, and walk and ride, in order to keep that *matter*, which I so mistakenly imagine my body 15 at present to consist of, in as good a plight as possible. Common sense (which in truth is very uncommon) is the best sense I know of. Abide by it: it will counsel you best. Read and hear for your amusement ingenious systems, nice questions sub- 20 tilely agitated, with all the refinements that warm imaginations suggest; but consider them only as exercitations for the mind, and return always to settle with common sense.

Letter XXIII

RULES FOR CONDUCT IN COMPANY

BATH, October the 19th, O. S. 1748. 25
DEAR BOY: Having in my last pointed out what sort of company you should keep, I will now give

4 Doctor Berkeley. George Berkeley. (1685-1753.) A celebrated English metaphysician.

you some rules for your conduct in it; rules which
my own experience and observation enable me to lay
down, and communicate to you with some degree of
confidence.   I have often given you hints of this kind
5 before, but then it has been by snatches; I will now
be more regular and methodical.   I shall say nothing
with regard to your bodily carriage and address, but
leave them to the care of your dancing-master, and
to your own attention to the best models: remember,
10 however, that they are of consequence.

Talk often, but never long; in that case, if you do
not please, at least you are sure not to tire your
hearers.   Pay your own reckoning, but do not treat
the whole company; this being one of the very few
15 cases in which people do not care to be treated, everyone being fully convinced that he has wherewithal to
pay.

Tell stories very seldom, and absolutely never but
where they are very apt and very short.   Omit every
20 circumstance that is not material, and beware of
digressions.   To have frequent recourse to narrative
betrays great want of imagination.

Never hold anybody by the button, or the hand,
in order to be heard out; for, if people are not willing
25 to hear you, you had much better hold your tongue
than them.

Most long talkers single out some one unfortunate
man in company (commonly him whom they observe
to be the most silent, or their next neighbor) to
30 whisper, or at least, in a half voice, to convey a continuity of words to.   This is excessively ill-bred, and,
in some degree, a fraud; conversation stock being a
joint and common property.   But, on the other hand,

if one of these unmerciful talkers lays hold of you,
hear him with patience (and at least seeming attention), if he is worth obliging; for nothing will oblige
him more than a patient hearing, as nothing would
hurt him more, than either to leave him in the midst 5
of his discourse, or to discover your impatience under
your affliction.

Take, rather than give, the tone of the company
you are in. If you have parts, you will show them,
more or less, upon every subject; and if you have 10
not, you had better talk sillily upon a subject of other
people's than of your own choosing.

Avoid as much as you can, in mixed companies,
argumentative, polemical conversations;   which
though they should not, yet certainly do, indispose, 15
for a time, the contending parties toward each other:
and, if the controversy grows warm and noisy,
endeavor to put an end to it by some genteel levity
or joke. I quieted such a conversation hubbub once,
by representing to them that though I was persuaded 20
none there present would repeat, out of company,
what passed in it, yet I could not answer for the discretion of the passengers in the street, who must
necessarily hear all that was said.

Above all things, and upon all occasions, avoid 25
speaking of yourself, if it be possible. Such is the
natural pride and vanity of our hearts, that it perpetually breaks out, even in people of the best parts,
in all the various modes and figures of the egotism.

Some abruptly speak advantageously of themselves, 30
without either pretense or provocation. They are
impudent. Others proceed more artfully, as they
imagine; and forge accusations against themselves,

complain of calumnies which they never heard, in
order to justify themselves, by exhibiting a catalogue
of their many virtues. They acknowledge it may,
indeed, seem odd, that they should talk in that manner
5 of themselves; it is what they do not like, and what
they never would have done; no, no tortures should
ever have forced it from them, if they had not been
thus unjustly and monstrously accused. But, in these
cases, justice is surely due to one's self, as well as to
10 others; and, when our character is attacked, we may
say, in our own justification, what otherwise we never
would have said. This thin veil of Modesty, drawn
before Vanity, is much too transparent to conceal it,
even from very moderate discernment.
15   Others go more modestly and more slyly still (as
they think) to work; but, in my mind, still more
ridiculously. They confess themselves (not without
some degree of shame and confusion) into all the
Cardinal Virtues; by first degrading them into weak-
20 nesses, and then owning their misfortune, in being
made up of those weaknesses. They cannot see
people suffer without sympathizing with, and endeavoring to help them. They cannot see people want
without relieving them: though truly their own cir-
25 cumstances cannot very well afford it. They cannot
help speaking truth, though they know all the impru-
dence of it. In short, they know that, with all these
weaknesses, they are not fit to live in the world, much
less to thrive in it. But they are now too old to
30 change, and must rub on as well as they can. This
sounds too ridiculous and *outré*, almost, for the stage;
and yet take my word for it, you will frequently meet
with it upon the common stage of the world. And

here I will observe, by the bye, that you will often
meet with characters in nature so extravagant, that a
discreet Poet would not venture to set them upon the
stage in their true and high coloring.

This principle of vanity and pride is so strong in 5
human nature, that it descends even to the lowest
objects; and one often sees people angling for praise,
where, admitting all they say to be true (which, by
the way, seldom is), no just praise is to be caught.
One man affirms that he has rode post a hundred 10
miles in six hours: probably it is a lie; but supposing
it to be true, what then? Why, he is a very good
postboy, that is all. Another asserts, and probably
not without oaths, that he has drunk six or eight
bottles of wine at a sitting: out of charity I will believe 15
him a liar; for if I do not I must think him a beast.

Such, and a thousand more, are the follies and
extravagances which vanity draws people into, and
which always defeat their own purpose: and, as Waller
says, upon another subject, 20

> " Make the wretch the most despised,
> Where most he wishes to be prized."

The only sure way of avoiding these evils is, never
to speak of yourself at all. But when historically you
are obliged to mention yourself, take care not to 25
drop one single word that can directly or indirectly
be construed as fishing for applause. Be your character what it will, it will be known; and nobody will
take it upon your own word. Never imagine that anything you can say yourself will varnish your defects, 30
or add luster to your perfections: but, on the con-

---

19 **Waller.** Edmund. (1605-1687.) An English panegyrical poet.

trary, it may, and nine times in ten will, make the former more glaring, and the latter obscure. If you are silent upon your own subject, neither envy, indignation, nor ridicule will obstruct or allay the applause
5 which you may really deserve; but if you publish your own panegyric, upon any occasion or in any shape whatsoever, and however artfully dressed or disguised, they will all conspire against you, and you will be disappointed of the very end you aim at.

10   Always look people in the face when you speak to them; the not doing it is thought to imply conscious guilt; besides that, you lose the advantage of observing by their countenances what impression your discourse makes upon them. In order to know people's
15 real sentiments, I trust much more to my eyes than to my ears; for they can say whatever they have a mind I should hear, but they can seldom help looking what they have no intention that I should know.

Neither retail nor receive scandal, willingly; for
20 though the defamation of others may, for the present, gratify the malignity or the pride of our hearts, cool reflection will draw very disadvantageous conclusions from such a disposition; and in the case of scandal, as in that of robbery, the receiver is always thought
25 as bad as the thief.

Mimicry, which is the common and favorite amusement of little, low minds, is in the utmost contempt with great ones. It is the lowest and most illiberal of all buffoonery. Pray neither practice it yourself,
30 nor applaud it in others. Besides that, the person mimicked is insulted; and, as I have often observed to you before, an insult is never forgiven.

I need not (I believe) advise you to adapt your

conversation to the people you are conversing with;
for I suppose you would not, without this caution,
have talked upon the same subject, and in the same
manner, to a Minister of State, a Bishop, a Philosopher, a Captain, and a Woman. A man of the world 5
must, like the Chameleon, be able to take every different hue; which is by no means a criminal or abject,
but a necessary complaisance, for it relates only to
Manners, and not to Morals.

One word only as to swearing; and that I hope 10
and believe is more than is necessary. You may
sometimes hear some people in good company inter-
lard their discourse with oaths, by the way of embel-
lishment, as they think; but you must observe, too,
that those who do so are never those who contribute, 15
in any degree, to give that company the denomination
of good company. They are always subalterns, or
people of low education; for that practice, besides
that is has no one temptation to plead, is as silly and
as illiberal as it is wicked.   20

Loud laughter is the mirth of the mob, who are
only pleased with silly things; for true Wit or good
Sense never excited a laugh since the creation of
the world. A man of parts and fashion is therefore
only seen to smile, but never heard to laugh.   25

But, to conclude this long letter; all the above-mentioned rules, however carefully you may observe them,
will lose half their effect if unaccompanied by the
Graces. Whatever you say, if you say it with a supercilious, cynical face, or an embarrassed countenance, 30
or a silly disconcerted grin, will be ill received. If, into
the bargain, *you mutter it, or utter it indistinctly and
ungracefully*, it will be still worse received. If your

air and address are vulgar, awkward, and *gauche*, you
may be esteemed indeed, if you have great intrinsic
merit, but you will never please; and without pleasing,
you will rise but heavily.   Venus, among the An-
5 cients, was synonymous with the Graces, who were
always supposed to accompany her; and Horace tells
us that even Youth, and Mercury, the God of Arts
and Eloquence, would not do without her.

" —Parum comis *sine te Juventas*
10   *Mercuriusque.*"

They are not inexorable Ladies, and may be had
if properly and diligently pursued.   Adieu.

Letter XXIV

THE GRACES: THE DUKE OF MARLBOROUGH

LONDON, November the 18th, O. S. 1748.
DEAR BOY: Whatever I see or whatever I hear, my
15 first consideration is, whether it can in any way be
useful to you.   As a proof of this, I went accidentally
the other day into a print-shop, where, among many
others, I found one print from a famous design of
Carlo Maratti, who died about thirty years ago, and
20 was the last eminent painter in Europe: the subject
is, *il Studio del Disegno;* or, the School of Drawing.
An old man, supposed to be the Master, points to
his Scholars, who are variously employed, in perspective, geometry, and the observation of the statues

---

¹ Gauche.   Literally, left, left-handed, hence abruptness of manner.
⁸ Parum . . . . Mercuriusque.   Horace, Odes, I. 30, 7.   "Youth and
Mercury less agreeable without thee."

of antiquity. With regard to perspective, of which
there are some little specimens, he has wrote, *Tanto
che basti*, that is, *As much as is sufficient;* with regard
to geometry, *Tanto che basti* again; with regard to
the contemplation of the ancient statues, there is 5
written, *Non mai a bastanza; There never can be enough.*
But in the clouds, at the top of the piece, are represented the three Graces; with this just sentence written
over them, *Senza di noi ogni fatica è vana;* that is,
Without us all labor is vain. This everybody allows 10
to be true, in painting; but all people do not seem
to consider, as I hope you will, that this truth is full
as applicable to every other art or science; indeed,
to everything that is to be said or done. I will send
you the print itself, by Mr. Eliot, when he returns. 15
    It must be owned that the Graces do not seem to
be natives of Great Britain, and I doubt the best of
us here have more of the rough than the polished dia-
mond. Since barbarism drove them out of Greece
and Rome, they seem to have taken refuge in France, 20
where their temples are numerous, and their worship
the established one. Examine yourself seriously, why
such and such people please and engage you, more
than such and such others of equal merit, and you
will always find, that it is because the former have 25
the Graces, and the latter not. I have known many
a woman with an exact shape, and a symmetrical
assemblage of beautiful features, please nobody; while
others, with very moderate shapes and features, have
charmed everybody. Why? because Venus will not 30
charm so much without her attendant Graces, as they
will without her. Among men how often have I seen
the most solid merit and knowledge neglected, unwel-

come, or even rejected, for want of them? While flimsy parts, little knowledge, and less merit, introduced by the Graces, have been received, cherished, and admired. Even virtue, which is moral beauty,
5 wants some of its charms, if unaccompanied by them.

If you ask me how you shall acquire what neither you nor I can define or ascertain, I can only answer, *By observation*. Form yourself, with regard to others, upon what you feel pleases you in them. I can tell
10 you the importance, the advantage, of having the Graces, but I cannot give them you: I heartily wish I could, and I certainly would; for I do not know a better present that I could make you. To show you that a very wise, philosophical, and retired man thinks
15 upon that subject as I do, who have always lived in the world, I send you, by Mr. Eliot, the famous Mr. Locke's book upon Education; in which you will find the stress that he lays upon the Graces, which he calls (and very truly) Good breeding. I have marked all the
20 parts of that book which are worth your attention; for as he begins with the child almost from its birth, the parts relative to its infancy would be useless to you. Germany is still less than England the seat of the Graces; however, you had as good not say so while
25 you are there. But the place which you are going to, in a great degree is, for I have known as many well-bred pretty men come from Turin as from any part of Europe. The late King Victor Amedée took great pains to form such of his subjects as were of any con-
30 sideration, both to business and manners; the present King, I am told, follows his example: this, however, is certain, that in all Courts and Congresses, where there are various foreign Ministers, those of the King

of Sardinia are generally the ablest, the politest, and *les plus déliés*. You will, therefore, at Turin, have very good models to form yourself upon; and remember, that with regard to the best models, as well as to the antique Greek statues in the print, *non mai* 5 *a bastanza*. Observe every word, look, and motion, of those who are allowed to be the most accomplished persons there. Observe their natural and careless, but genteel air; their unembarrassed good breeding; their unassuming, but yet unprostituted, dignity. 10 Mind their decent mirth, their discreet frankness, and that *entregent*, which, as much above the frivolous as below the important and the secret, is the proper medium for conversation in mixed companies. I will observe, by the bye, that the talent of that light *entre-* 15 *gent* is often of great use to a foreign Minister; not only as it helps him to domesticate himself in many families, but also as it enables him to put by and parry some subjects of conversation, which might possibly lay him under difficulties, both what to say and 20 how to look.

Of all the men that ever I knew in my life (and I knew him extremely well), the late Duke of Marlborough possessed the Graces in the highest degree, not to say engrossed them; and indeed he got the 25 most by them; for I will venture (contrary to the custom of profound historians, who always assign deep causes for great events) to ascribe the better half of the Duke of Marlborough's greatness and

---

5 Le plus déliés. The shrewdest.
11 Entregent. Tact.
22 Duke of Marlborough. (1650-1722.) His wealth, power, and fame were due to his tact and skill in managing men, to the influence of his wife, and to his marvelous military genius. '' But courage and skill in arms did less for Marl-

riches to those Graces. He was eminently illiterate;
wrote bad English, and spelled it still worse. He
had no share of what is commonly called *Parts;* that
is, he had no brightness, nothing shining in his genius.
5 He had, most undoubtedly, an excellent good plain
understanding, with sound judgment. But these
alone would probably have raised him but something
higher than they found him, which was Page to King
James the Second's Queen. There the Graces pro-
10 tected and promoted him; for, while he was an Ensign
of the Guards, the Duchess of Cleveland, then favorite
mistress to King Charles the Second, struck by those
very Graces, gave him five thousand pounds; with
which he immediately bought an annuity for his life,
15 of five hundred pounds a year, of my grandfather,
Halifax, which was the foundation of his subsequent
fortune. His figure was beautiful; but his manner
was irresistible, by either man or woman. It was by
this engaging, graceful manner that he was enabled,
20 during all this war, to connect the various and jarring
Powers of the Grand Alliance, and to carry them on

borough on his return to the English court than his personal beauty . . . . and his
manners were as winning as his person."—*J. R. Green.* His wife, Sarah Jennings,
was the intimate friend of Queen Anne, and was often called " Queen Sarah."
" Queen Anne only reigned, while Queen Sarah governed."—*Temple Bar.* Marlborough was chief of the triumvirate composed of himself, Prince Eugene, and
Heinsius, the Grand Pensionary of Amsterdam : and was the general in chief of
the combined English and Dutch armies in the war with France. Chesterfield
exaggerates his influence over his colleagues : had it been greater, their victories
would have been greater. Marlborough was a traitor to James II. and to William.
" So notorious was his treason that on the eve of the French invasion of 1692 he
was one of the first of the suspected persons to be sent to the Tower."—*J. R. Green.*

16 Halifax. George Savile, Marquis of Halifax. (1630-1695.) Statesman,
orator, author : not to be confounded with Charles Montague, Earl of Halifax,
(1661-1715), the financier, author of the bill establishing the Bank of England.

21 Powers of the Grand Alliance. The Grand Alliance was signed May
12, 1689, and included England, Germany, and Holland ; afterward, Spain and
Savoy, also. Its object was to prevent the union of France and Spain.

to the main object of the war, notwithstanding their
private and separate views, jealousies, and wrong-
headednesses. Whatever Court he went to (and he
was often obliged to go himself to some resty and
refractory ones), he as constantly prevailed, and 5
brought them into his measures. The Pensionary
Heinsius, a venerable old Minister, grown gray in
business, and who had governed the Republic of the
United Provinces for more than forty years, was absolutely governed by the Duke of Marlborough, as that 10
Republic feels to this day. He was always cool; and
nobody ever observed the least variation in his
countenance: he could refuse more gracefully than
other people could grant; and those who went away
from him the most dissatisfied, as to the substance 15
of their business, were yet personally charmed with
him, and, in some degree, comforted by his manner.
With all his gentleness and gracefulness, no man living was more conscious of his situation, nor maintained his dignity better.   20

Letter XXV

DIGNITY OF MANNERS

LONDON, Aug. 10, O. S. 1749.

   •   •   •   •   •   •   •

There is a certain dignity of manners absolutely
necessary to make even the most valuable character
either respected or respectable.

Horse-play, romping, frequent and loud fits of 25
laughter, jokes, waggery, and indiscriminate familiarity will sink both merit and knowledge into a degree

of contempt.   They compose at most a merry fellow,
and a merry fellow was never yet a respectable man.
Indiscriminate familiarity either offends your superiors, or else dubs you their dependent and led cap-
5 tain.   It gives your inferiors just but troublesome
and improper claims of equality.   A joker is near
akin to a buffoon, and neither of them is the nearest
related to wit.   Whoever is either admitted or sought
for in company upon any other account than that
10 of his merit and manners, is never respected there
but only made use of. We will have such-a-one, for he
sings prettily; we will invite such-a-one to a ball, for
he dances well; we will have such-a-one at supper, for
he is always joking and laughing; we will ask another
15 because he plays deep at all games, or because he
can drink a great deal.   These are all vilifying dis-
tinctions, mortifying preference, and exclude all ideas
of esteem and regard.   Whoever *is had* (as it is called)
in company for the sake of any one thing singly, is
20 singly that thing, and will never be considered in
any other light; consequently never respected, let his
merits be what they will.

   This dignity of manners which I recommend so
much to you is not only as different from pride as
25 true courage is from blustering, or true wit from
joking, but is absolutely inconsistent with it; for
nothing vilifies and degrades more than pride.   The
pretensions of the proud man are oftener treated with
sneer and contempt than with indignation; as we offer
30 ridiculously too little to a tradesman who asks ridiculously too much for his goods, but we do not haggle
with one who only asks a just and reasonable price.

   Abject flattery and indiscriminate assentation degrade as much as indiscriminate contradiction and noisy debate disgust. But a modest assertion of one's own opinion and a complaisant acquiescence in other people's preserve dignity.

Vulgar, low expressions, awkward motions and [5] address, vilify; as they imply either a very low turn of mind or low education and low company.

Frivolous curiosity about trifles and laborious attention to little objects, which neither require nor deserve a moment's thought, lower a man, who from [10] thence is thought (and not unjustly) incapable of greater matters. Cardinal de Retz very sagaciously marked out Cardinal Chigi for a little mind from the moment that he told him he had wrote three years with the same pen, and that it was an excellent good [15] one still.

· · · · · · ·

Letter XXVI

"COMPLETE THE WORK"

LONDON, September the 12th, O. S. 1749.

DEAR BOY: It seems extraordinary, but it is very true, that my anxiety for you increases in proportion to the good accounts which I receive of you from all [20] hands. I promise myself so much from you, that I dread the least disappointment. You are now so near the port, which I have so long wished and labored to bring you into, that my concern would be doubled should you be shipwrecked within sight of [25]

---

[12] **Cardinal de Retz.** (1614-1679.) An able French politician and diplomatist. He was largely responsible for the war of the Fronde, which began in 1648.

[13] **Cardinal Chigi.** An Italian prelate, member of a noted family.

it. The object, therefore, of this letter is (laying aside
all the authority of a parent), to conjure you as a
friend, by the affection you have for me (and surely
you have reason to have some), and by the regard
5 you have for yourself, to go on, with assiduity and
attention, to complete that work, which, of late, you
have carried on so well, and which is now so near
being finished. My wishes, and my plan, were to
make you shine, and distinguish yourself equally in
10 the learned and the polite world. Few have been able
to do it. Deep learning is generally tainted with
pedantry, or at least unadorned by manners; as, on
the other hand, polite manners, and the turn of the
world, are too often unsupported by knowledge, and
15 consequently end contemptibly in the frivolous dissipation of drawing rooms. You are now got over the
dry and difficult parts of learning; what remains
requires much more time than trouble. You have
lost time by your illness; you must regain it now or
20 never. I therefore most earnestly desire, for your
own sake, that for these next six months, at least six
hours every morning, uninterruptedly, may be inviolably sacred to your studies with Mr. Harte. I do
not know whether he will require so much, but I
25 know that I do, and hope you will, and consequently
prevail with him to give you that time: I own it is a
good deal; but when both you and he consider, that
the work will be so much better and so much sooner
done, by such an assiduous and continued applica-
30 tion, you will neither of you think it too much, and
each will find his account in it. So much for the
mornings which, from your own good sense, and Mr.
Harte's tenderness and care of you, will, I am sure,

be thus well employed. It is not only reasonable,
but useful, too, that your evenings should be devoted
to amusements and pleasures; and therefore I not
only allow, but recommend, that they should be
employed at assemblies, balls, *spectacles*, and in the 5
best companies; with this restriction only, that the
consequences of the evening's diversions may not
break in upon the morning's studies, by breakfastings,
visits, and idle parties into the country. At your age,
you need not be ashamed, when any of these morn- 10
ing parties are proposed, to say you must beg to be
excused, for you are obliged to devote your mornings
to Mr. Harte; that I will have it so; and that you dare
not do otherwise. Lay it all upon me, though I am
persuaded it will be as much your own inclination as 15
is mine. But those frivolous, idle people, whose
time hangs upon their own hands, and who desire to
make others lose theirs too, are not to be reasoned
with; and indeed it would be doing them too much
honor. The shortest civil answers are the best; *I* 20
cannot, I dare not, instead of *I will not;* for, if you were
to enter with them into the necessity of study, and the
usefulness of knowledge, it would only furnish them
with matter for their silly jests; which, though I
would not have you mind, I would not have you 25
invite. I will suppose you at Rome, studying six
hours uninterruptedly with Mr. Harte, every morning,
and passing your evenings with the best company of
Rome, observing their manners, and forming your
own; and I will suppose a number of idle, saunter- 30
ing, illiterate English, as there commonly is there,
living entirely with one another, supping, drinking,
and sitting up late at each other's lodgings; com-

monly in riots and scrapes when drunk; and never
in good company when sober. I will take one of
these pretty fellows, and give you the dialogue between him and yourself; such as I dare say it will be
5 on his side, and such as I hope it will be on yours.

Englishman. Will you come and breakfast with me
to-morrow; there will be four or five of our countrymen; we have provided chaises, and we will drive
somewhere out of town after breakfast?
10   *Stanhope.* I am very sorry I cannot, but I am
obliged to be at home all morning.
Englishman. Why, then, we will come and breakfast with you.
Stanhope. I can't do that neither, I am engaged.
15   *Englishman.* Well, then, let it be the next day.
Stanhope. To tell you the truth, it can be no day in
the morning, for I neither go out nor see anybody at
home before twelve.
Englishman. And what the devil do you do with
20 yourself till twelve o'clock?
Stanhope. I am not by myself, I am with Mr. Harte.
Englishman. Then what the devil do you do with
him?
Stanhope. We study different things; we read, we
25 converse.
Englishman. Very pretty amusement indeed! Are
you to take Orders, then?
Stanhope. Yes, my father's orders, I believe, I must
take.
30   *Englishman.* Why, hast thou no more spirit than to
mind an old fellow a thousand miles off?
Stanhope. If I don't mind his orders he won't mind
my draughts.

Englishman. What, does the old prig threaten, then? threatened folks live long; never mind threats.

Stanhope. No, I can't say that he has ever threatened me in his life; but I believe I had best not provoke him. 5

Englishman. Pooh! you would have one angry letter from the old fellow, and there would be an end of it.

Stanhope. You mistake him mightily; he always does more than he says. He has never been angry 10 with me yet, that I remember, in his life; but if I were to provoke him I am sure he would never forgive me; he would be coolly immovable, and I might beg and pray, and write my heart out to no purpose.

Englishman. Why, then, he is an old dog, that's all 15 I can say; and pray, are you to obey your dry-nurse too, this same, what's his name—Mr. Harte?

Stanhope. Yes.

Englishman. So he stuffs you all morning with Greek, and Latin, and Logic, and all that. Egad, I 20 have a dry-nurse, too, but I never looked into a book with him in my life; I have not so much as seen the face of him this week, and don't care a louse if I never see it again.

Stanhope. My dry-nurse never desires anything of 25 me that is not reasonable and for my own good, and therefore I like to be with him.

Englishman. Very sententious and edifying, upon my word! at this rate you will be reckoned a very good young man. 30

Stanhope. Why, that will do me no harm.

Englishman. Will you be with us to-morrow in the evening, then? We shall be ten with you, and I have

got some excellent good wine, and we'll be very
merry.

Stanhope. I am very much obliged to you, but I am
engaged for all the evening to-morrow; first at Car-
5 dinal Albani's, and then to sup at the Venetian
Embassadress's.

Englishman. How the devil can you like being
always with these foreigners? I never go amongst
them, with all their formalities and ceremonies. I
10 am never easy in company with them, and I don't
know why, but I am ashamed.

Stanhope. I am neither ashamed nor afraid; I am
very easy with them; they are very easy with me; I
get the language, and I see their characters by con-
15 versing with them; and that is what we are sent
abroad for. Is it not?

Englishman. I hate your modest women's company; your women of fashion, as they call 'em. I
don't know what to say to them, for my part.

20 *Stanhope.* Have you ever conversed with them?

Englishman. No. I never conversed with them;
but I have been sometimes in their company, though
much against my will.

Stanhope. But at least they have done you no hurt,
25 which is, probably, more than you can say of the
women you do converse with.

Englishman. That's true, I own; but for all that, I
would rather keep company with my surgeon half the
year than with your women of fashion the year round.

30 *Stanhope.* Tastes are different, you know, and every
man follows his own.

Englishman. That's true; but thine's a devilish odd
one, Stanhope. All morning with thy dry-nurse, all

the evening in formal fine company, and all day
long afraid of old Daddy in England. Thou art a
queer fellow, and I am afraid there's nothing to be
made of thee.

Stanhope. I am afraid so too.   5

Englishman. Well then, good-night to you; you
have no objection, I hope, to my being drunk to-
night, which I certainly will be.

Stanhope. Not in the least; nor to your being sick
to-morrow, which you as certainly will be; and so 10
good-night too.

You will observe that I have not put into your
mouth those good arguments which upon such an
occasion would, I am sure, occur to you, as piety and 15
affection toward me, regard and friendship for Mr.
Harte, respect for your own moral character, and for
all the relative duties of Man, Son, Pupil, and Citizen.
Such solid arguments would be thrown away upon
such shallow puppies. Leave them to their ignor- 20
ance, and to their dirty, disgraceful vices. They will
severely feel the effects of them, when it will be too
late. Without the comfortable refuge of learning,
and with all the sickness and pains of a ruined
stomach, and a rotten carcass, if they happen to arrive 25
at old age, it is an uneasy and ignominious one. The
ridicule which such fellows endeavor to throw upon
those who are not like them is, in the opinion of all
men of sense, the most authentic panegyric. Go on,
then, my dear child, in the way you are in, only for a 30
year and a half more; that is all I ask of you. After
that, I promise that you shall be your own master, and
that I will pretend to no other title than that of your

best and truest friend. You shall receive advice, but
no orders, from me; and in truth you will want no
other advice but such as youth and inexperience must
necessarily require. You shall certainly want noth-
5 ing that is requisite, not only for your conveniency,
but also for your pleasures, which I always desire
should be gratified. You will suppose that I mean
the pleasures *d'un honnête homme.*

Letter XXVII

LOW COMPANY

LONDON, September the 27th, O. S. 1749.
10   DEAR BOY: A vulgar, ordinary way of thinking,
acting, or speaking, implies a low education, and a
habit of low company. Young people contract it at
school, or among servants, with whom they are too
often used to converse; but, after they frequent good
15 company, they must want attention and observation
very much, if they do not lay it quite aside. And indeed if they do not, good company will be very apt
to lay them aside. The various kinds of vulgarisms
are infinite; I cannot pretend to point them out to
20 you; but I will give you some samples, by which you
may guess at the rest.
   A vulgar man is captious and jealous; eager and
impetuous about trifles. He suspects himself to be
slighted, thinks everything that is said meant at him;
25 if the company happens to laugh, he is persuaded they

---

* D'un honnête homme. Of an honorable man.

laugh at him; he grows angry and testy, says something very impertinent, and draws himself into a
scrape, by showing what he calls a proper spirit, and
asserting himself. A man of fashion does not suppose himself to be either the sole or principal object 5
of the thoughts, looks, or words of the company; and
never suspects that he is either slighted or laughed at,
unless he is conscious that he deserves it. And if
(which very seldom happens) the company is absurd
or ill-bred enough to do either, he does not care two- 10
pence, unless the insult be so gross and plain as to
require satisfaction of another kind. As he is above
trifles, he is never vehement and eager about them;
and, wherever they are concerned, rather acquiesces
than wrangles. A vulgar man's conversation always 15
savors strongly of the lowness of his education and
company. It turns chiefly upon his domestic affairs,
his servants, the excellent order he keeps in his own
family, and the little anecdotes of the neighborhood;
all which he relates with emphasis, as interesting 20
matters. He is a man gossip.

Vulgarism in language is the next and distinguishing characteristic of bad company and a bad education. A man of fashion avoids nothing with more
care than that. Proverbial expressions and trite say- 25
ings are the flowers of the rhetoric of a vulgar man.
Would he say that men differ in their tastes, he both
supports and adorns that opinion by the good old
saying, as he respectfully calls it, that *what is one man's
Meat is another man's Poison*. If anybody attempts 30
being *smart*, as he calls it, upon him, he gives them
Tit for Tat, ay, that he does. He has always some
favorite word for the time being, which, for the sake

of using often, he commonly abuses.   Such as *vastly*
angry, *vastly* kind, *vastly* handsome, and *vastly* ugly.
Even his pronunciation of proper words carries the
mark of the beast along with it.   He calls the earth
5 *yearth;* he is *obleiged*, not *obliged* to you.   He goes *to
wards* and not towards such a place.   He sometimes
affects hard words, by way of ornament, which he
always mangles like a learned woman.   A man of
fashion never has recourse to proverbs and vulgar
10 aphorisms, uses neither favorite words nor hard
words; but takes great care to speak very correctly
and grammatically, and to pronounce properly; that
is, according to the usage of the best companies.

Letter XXVIII

STYLE

LONDON, November the 24th, O. S. 1749.
15 DEAR BOY: Every rational being (I take it for
granted) proposes to himself some object more important than mere respiration and obscure animal
existence.   He desires to distinguish himself among
his fellow-creatures; and, *alicui negotio intentus,*
20 *præclari facinoris, aut artis bonæ famam quærit.*
Cæsar, when embarking in a storm, said that it was
not necessary he should live, but that it was absolutely necessary he should get to the place to which
he was going.   And Pliny leaves mankind this only

---

[1] **Vastly.**   The American, with equal impropriety, says *awful: awfully
nice*, etc.

[19] **Alicui . . . . quærit.**   "Devoting himself to a specialty, he seeks the
renown of a brilliant achievement or of great virtue."

alternative; either of doing what deserves to be
written, or of writing what deserves to be read. As
for those who do neither, *eorum vitam mortemque juxta
æstumo; quoniam de utraque siletur.* You have, I am
convinced, one or both of these objects in view; but 5
you must know and use the necessary means or your
pursuit will be vain and frivolous. In either case,
sapere est principium et fons; but it is by no means all.
That knowledge must be adorned, it must have luster
as well as weight, or it will be oftener taken for Lead 10
than for Gold. Knowledge you have, and will have:
I am easy upon that article. But my business, as
your friend, is not to compliment you upon what you
have, but to tell you with freedom what you want;
and I must tell you plainly that I fear you want every- 15
thing but knowledge.

I have written to you so often of late upon Good
Breeding, Address, *les Manières liantes*, the Graces,
etc., that I shall confine this letter to another subject,
pretty near akin to them, and which, I am sure, you 20
are full as deficient in; I mean, Style.

Style is the dress of thoughts; and let them be ever
so just, if your style is homely, coarse, and vulgar,

---

3 Eorum . . . . siletur. Sallust's *Catiline*, 2, 8. "I consider their lives
and deaths equally worthless, since no memorial remains of either." (Scribendi
recte) **sapere est et principium et fons.** Horace: *Ars Poetica*, 309. "Wisdom
is both the beginning and the constant source of good composition"). Wickham
says this line is the motto of the *Ars Poetica*. Howes renders it.

> "In the philosophy of man to excel
> Is the prime root and spring of writing well."

Byron paraphrases it thus :

> "Though modern practice sometimes differs quite,
> 'Tis just as well to think before you write."

Another writer :

> "Good writing begins in good thinking."

18 Les Maniéres liantes. Easy manners.

they will appear to as much disadvantage, and be as
ill received, as your person, though ever so well-
proportioned, would if dressed in rags, dirt, and
tatters.   It is not every understanding that can judge
5 of matter; but every ear can and does judge, more or
less, of style: and were I either to speak or write to
the public, I should prefer moderate matter, adorned
with all the beauties and elegancies of style, to the
strongest matter in the world, ill worded and ill
10 delivered.

You have with you three or four of the best English Authors, Dryden, Atterbury, and Swift; read
them with the utmost care, and with a particular
view to their language; and they may possibly cor-
15 rect that *curious infelicity of diction*, which you acquired at Westminster.   Mr. Harte excepted, I will
admit that you have met with very few English
abroad, who could improve your style; and with
many, I dare say, who speak as ill as yourself, and it
20 may be worse; you must, therefore, take the more
pains, and consult your authors, and Mr. Harte, the
more.   I need not tell you how attentive the Romans
and Greeks, particularly the Athenians, were to this
object.   It is also a study among the Italians and the
25 French, witness their respective Academies and Dic-
tionaries, for improving and fixing their languages.
To our shame be it spoken, it is less attended to here
than in any polite country; but that is no reason why
you should not attend to it; on the contrary, it will
30 distinguish you the more.   Cicero says, very truly,
that it is glorious to excel other men in that very
article, in which men excel brutes; *speech.*

Constant experience has shown me, that great

purity and elegance of style, with a graceful elocution,
cover a multitude of faults, in either a speaker or a
writer. For my own part, I confess (and I believe
most people are of my mind) that if a speaker should
ungracefully mutter or stammer out to me the sense 5
of an angel, deformed by barbarisms and solecisms,
or larded with vulgarisms, he should never speak to
me a second time, if I could help it. Gain the heart,
or you gain nothing; the eyes and the ears are the
only roads to the heart. Merit and knowledge will 10
not gain hearts, though they will secure them when
gained. Pray have that truth ever in your mind.
Engage the eyes, by your address, air, and motions;
soothe the ears, by the elegancy and harmony of your
diction: the heart will certainly follow; and the whole 15
man, or woman, will as certainly follow the heart. I
must repeat it to you, over and over again, that, with
all the knowledge which you may have at present, or
hereafter acquire, and with all the merit that ever man
had, if you have not a graceful address, liberal and 20
engaging manners, a prepossessing air, and a good
degree of eloquence in speaking and writing, you will
be nobody: but will have the daily mortification of
seeing people, with not one-tenth part of your merit
or knowledge, get the start of you, and disgrace you, 25
both in company and in business.

Letter XXIX

" A TONGUE TO PERSUADE "

LONDON, December the 12th, O. S. 1749.

DEAR BOY: Lord Clarendon, in his history, says of
Mr. John Hampden, *that he had a head to contrive, a
tongue to persuade, and a hand to execute any mischief.*
5 I shall not now enter into the justness of this character of Mr. Hampden, to whose brave stand against
the illegal demand of ship-money we owe our present
liberties; but I mention it to you as the character
which, with the alteration of one single word, *Good,*
10 instead of *Mischief,* I would have you aspire to, and
use your utmost endeavors to deserve. The head to
contrive, God must to a certain degree have given
you; but it is in your own power greatly to improve
it by study, observation, and reflection. As for the
15 *tongue to persuade,* it wholly depends upon yourself;
and without it the best head will contrive to very
little purpose. The hand to execute depends, likewise, in my opinion, in a great measure upon yourself.
Serious reflection will always give courage in a good
20 cause; and the courage arising from reflection is of
a much superior nature to the animal and constitutional courage of a foot soldier. The former is steady
and unshaken, where the *nodus* is *dignus vindice;* the
latter is oftener improperly than properly exerted, but .
25 always brutally.

---

²³ Nodus (literally *knot,* here *difficult*). Dignus vindice. Worthy of a pro-
tector. Lord Chesterfield had in mind, doubtless : " Nec deus intersit, nisi dignus
vindice nodus inciderit." Horace : *Ars Poetica,* 191. " Nor let a god interfere,
unless a difficulty presents itself worthy of a god's unraveling."

The second member of my text (to speak eccle-siastically, shall be the subject of my following discourse; *the tongue to persuade*. As judicious Preachers recommend those virtues which they think their several audiences want the most: such as truth 5 and continence at Court; disinterestedness in the City; and sobriety in the Country.

You must certainly, in the course of your little experience, have felt the different effects of elegant and inelegant speaking. Do you not suffer when 10 people accost you in a stammering or hesitating man-ner: in an untuneful voice, with false accents and cadences; puzzling and blundering through sole-cisms, barbarisms, and vulgarisms; misplacing even their bad words, and inverting all method? Does not 15 this prejudice you against their matter, be it what it will; nay, even against their persons? I am sure it does me. On the other hand, do you not feel your-self inclined, prepossessed, nay, even engaged in favor of those who address you in the direct contrary man- 20 ner? The effects of a correct and adorned style of method and perspicuity, are incredible toward per-suasion; they often supply the want of reason and argument, but when used in the support of reason and argument they are irresistible. The French 25 attend very much to the purity and elegancy of their style, even in common conversation; insomuch that it is a character, to say of a man, *qu'il narre bien*. Their conversations frequently turn upon the deli-cacies of their language, and an Academy is employed 30 in fixing it. The *Crusca*, in Italy, has the same

---

[28] Qu'il narre bien. How well he tells a story.
[31] Crusca. The *Accademia della Crusca*, corresponding to the French Academy.

object; and I have met with very few Italians who
did not speak their own language correctly and elegantly. How much more necessary is it for an Englishman to do so who is to speak it in a public
5 assembly, where the laws and liberties of his country
are the subjects of his deliberation? The tongue that
would persuade there must not content itself with
mere articulation. You know what pains Demosthenes took to correct his naturally bad elocution;
10 you know that he declaimed by the seaside in storms,
to prepare himself for the noise of the tumultuous
assemblies he was to speak to; and you can now
judge of the correctness and elegancy of his style.
He thought all these things of consequence, and he
15 thought right; pray do you think so too. It is of the
utmost consequence to you to be of that opinion. If
you have the least defect in your elocution, take the
utmost care and pains to correct it. Do not neglect
your style, whatever language you speak in, or whom-
20 ever you speak to, were it your footman. Seek
always for the best words and the happiest expressions you can find. Do not content yourself with
being barely understood; but adorn your thoughts,
and dress them as you would your person; which,
25 however well proportioned it might be, it would be
very improper and indecent to exhibit naked, or even
worse dressed than people of your sort are.

Letter XXX

PURITY OF CHARACTER

LONDON, January the 8th, Q. S. 1750.

DEAR BOY: I have seldom or never written to you
upon the subject of Religion and Morality: your own
reason, I am persuaded, has given you true notions
of both; they speak best for themselves; but, if they 5
wanted assistance, you have Mr. Harte at hand, both
for precept and example: to your own reason, therefore, and to Mr. Harte, shall I refer you, for the
Reality of both; and confine myself, in this letter, to
the decency, the utility, and the necessity of scrupu- 10
lously preserving the appearances of both.   When I
say the appearances of religion, I do not mean that
you should talk or act like a Missionary, or an Enthu-
siast, nor that you should take up a controversial
cudgel against whoever attacks the sect you are of; 15
this would be both useless, and unbecoming your age:
but I mean that you should by no means seem to
approve, encourage, or applaud, those libertine
notions, which strike at religions equally, and which
are the poor threadbare topics of half Wits, and 20
minute Philosophers.   Even those who are silly
enough to laugh at their jokes are still wise enough
to distrust and detest their characters: for, putting
moral virtues at the highest, and religion at the
lowest, religion must still be allowed to be a collateral 25
security, at least, to Virtue; and every prudent man
will sooner trust to two securities than to one.
Whenever, therefore, you happen to be in company

with those pretended *Esprits forts*,¹ or with thoughtless libertines, who laugh at all religion to show their
wit, or disclaim it to complete their riot, let no word
or look of yours intimate the least approbation; on
5 the contrary, let a silent gravity express your dislike:
but enter not into the subject, and decline such un-
profitable and indecent controversies. Depend upon
this truth, That every man is the worse looked upon,
and the less trusted, for being thought to have no
10 religion; in spite of all the pompous and specious
epithets he may assume, of *Esprit fort*, Free-thinker,
or Moral Philosopher; and a wise Atheist (if such a
thing there is) would, for his own interest, and character in this world, pretend to some religion.
15   Your moral character must be not only pure, but,
like Cæsar's wife, unsuspected. The least speck or
blemish upon it is fatal. Nothing degrades and vilifies more, for it excites and unites detestation and
contempt. There are, however, wretches in the
20 world profligate enough to explode all notions of
moral good and evil; to maintain that they are merely
local, and depend entirely upon the customs and
fashions of different countries: nay, there are still, if
possible, more unaccountable wretches; I mean those
25 who affect to preach and propagate such absurd and
infamous notions, without believing them themselves.
These are the devil's hypocrites. Avoid, as much as
possible, the company of such people; who reflect a
degree of discredit and infamy upon all who converse
30 with them. But as you may sometimes, by accident,
fall into such company, take great care that no complaisance, no good-humor, no warmth of festal mirth,

---

¹ **Esprits forts.** Strong-minded men.

ever make you seem even to acquiesce, much less to approve or applaud, such infamous doctrines. On the other hand, do not debate, nor enter into serious argument, upon a subject so much below it: but content yourself with telling these *Apostles*, that you know 5 they are not serious; that you have a much better opinion of them than they would have you have; and that you are very sure they would not practice the doctrine they preach. But put your private mark upon them, and shun them forever afterward. 10

There is nothing so delicate as your Moral character, and nothing which it is your interest so much to preserve pure. Should you be suspected of Injustice, Malignity, Perfidy, Lying, etc., all the parts and knowledge in the world will never procure you 15 esteem, friendship, or respect. A strange concurrence of circumstances has sometimes raised very bad men to high stations; but they have been raised like criminals to a pillory, where their persons and their crimes, by being more conspicuous, are only the more 20 known, the more detested, and the more pelted and insulted. If, in any case whatsoever, affectation and ostentation are pardonable, it is in the case of morality; though, even there, I would not advise you to a pharisaical pomp of virtue. But I will recom- 25 mend to you a most scrupulous tenderness for your moral character, and the utmost care not to say or do the least thing that may, ever so slightly, taint it. Show yourself, upon all occasions, the advocate, the friend, but not the bully, of Virtue. Colonel Chartres, 30 whom you have certainly heard of (who was, I believe, the most notorious blasted rascal in the world, and who had, by all sorts of crimes, amassed immense

wealth), was so sensible of the disadvantage of a bad
character, that I heard him once say, in his impudent,
profligate manner, that though he would not give one
farthing for Virtue, he would give ten thousand
5 pounds for a character; because he should get a hundred thousand pounds by it; whereas he was so
blasted that he had no longer an opportunity of cheat-
ing people. Is it possible, then, that an honest man
can neglect what a wise rogue would purchase so
10 dear?

There is one of the vices above-mentioned, into
which people of good education, and, in the main, of
good principles, sometimes fall, from mistaken
notions of skill, dexterity, and self-defense; I mean
15 Lying: though it is inseparably attended with more
infamy and loss than any other. The prudence and
necessity of often concealing the truth insensibly
seduces people to violate it. It is the only art of
mean capacities, and the only refuge of mean spirits.
20 Whereas concealing the truth, upon proper occasions,
is as prudent and as innocent, as telling a lie, upon
any occasion, is infamous and foolish. I will state you
a case in your own department. Suppose you are
employed at a foreign Court, and that the Minister of
25 that Court is absurd or impertinent enough to ask
you what your instructions are; will you tell him a
lie; which, as soon as found out, and found out it
certainly will be, must destroy your credit, blast your
character, and render you useless there? No. Will
30 you tell him the truth, then, and betray your trust?
As certainly, No. But you will answer, with firmness, That you are surprised at such a question; that
1 are persuaded he does not expect an answer to

it; but that, at all events, he certainly will not have one. Such an answer will give him confidence in you; he will conceive an opinion of your veracity, of which opinion you may afterward make very honest and fair advantages. But if, in negotiations, you are 5 looked upon as a liar, and a trickster, no confidence will be placed in you, nothing will be communicated to you, and you will be in the situation of a man who has been burnt in the cheek; and who, from that mark, cannot afterward get an honest livelihood, if he 10 would, but must continue a thief.

Lord Bacon very justly makes a distinction between Simulation and Dissimulation; and allows the latter rather than the former: but still observes, that they are the weaker sort of Politicians who have 15 recourse to either. A man who has strength of mind, and strength of parts, wants neither of them. " Certainly (says he) the ablest men that ever were have all had an openness and frankness of dealing, and a name of certainty and veracity; but then they were like 20 horses well managed; for they could tell, passing well, when to stop, or turn: and at such times, when they thought the case indeed required some dissimulation, if then they used it, it came to pass that the former opinion spread abroad, of their good faith and 25 clearness of dealing, made them almost invisible." There are people who indulge themselves in a sort of lying, which they reckon innocent, and which in one sense is so; for it hurts nobody but themselves. This

---

12 **Lord Bacon.** Lord Bacon also says : " It will be acknowledged even by those that practice it not, that clear and sound dealing is the honor of man's nature, and that mixture of falsehood is like alloy in coin of gold and silver, which may make the metal work the better, but it embaseth [debases] it. There is no vice that doth so cover a man with shame as to be found false and perfidious."

sort of lying is the spurious offspring of vanity, be-
gotten upon folly: these people deal in the marvelous;
they have seen some things that never existed; they
have seen other things which they never really saw,
5 though they did exist, only because they were thought
worth seeing. Has anything remarkable been said
or done in any place, or in any company? they immediately present and declare themselves eye or ear
witnesses of it. They have done feats themselves,
10 unattempted, or at least unperformed, by others.
They are always the heroes of their own fables; and
think that they gain consideration, or at least present
attention, by it. Whereas, in truth, all they get is
ridicule and contempt, not without a good degree of
15 distrust: for one must naturally conclude, that he
who will tell any lie from idle vanity, will not scruple
telling a greater for interest. Had I really seen anything so very extraordinary as to be almost incredible,
I would keep it to myself, rather than, by telling it,
20 give any one body room to doubt for one minute my
veracity. For God's sake, be scrupulously jealous of
the purity of your moral character; keep it immacu-
late, unblemished, unsullied; and it will be unsuspected. Defamation and calumny never attack, where
25 there is no weak place; they magnify, but they do not
create.

There is a very great difference between that purity
of character, which I so earnestly recommend to you,
and the Stoical gravity and austerity of character,
30 which I do by no means recommend to you. At your
age, I would no more wish you to be a Cato, than a
Clodius. Be, and be reckoned, a man of pleasure,

---

32 **Clodius.** Publius Clodius (or Claudius) Pulcher, " one of the most profligate

as well as a man of business. Enjoy this happy and
giddy time of your life; shine in the pleasures and
in the company of people of your own age. This
is all to be done, and indeed only can be done, without the least taint to the purity of your moral char- 5
acter: for those mistaken young fellows, who think
to shine by an impious or immoral licentiousness,
shine only from their stinking, like corrupted flesh,
in the dark. Without this purity, you can have no
dignity of character, and without dignity of character 10
it is impossible to rise in the world. You must be
respectable, if you will be respected. I have known
people slattern away their character, without really
polluting it; the consequence of which has been, that
they have become innocently contemptible; their 15
merit has been dimmed, their pretensions unregarded,
and all their views defeated. Character must be kept
bright, as well as clean. Content yourself with
mediocrity in nothing. In purity of character, and
in politeness of manners, labor to excel all, if you wish 20
to equal many. Adieu.

Letter XXXI

ECONOMY OF TIME: DISPATCH OF BUSINESS

LONDON, February the 5th, O. S. 1750.
MY DEAR FRIEND: Very few people are good
economists of their Fortune, and still fewer of their

---

characters of a profligate age." He was a contemporary and an enemy of Cicero.
Lord Chesterfield does injustice to Cato, who was intensely patriotic, and, in morals,
far in advance of his age.

²⁸ Observe the change of address ; hereafter it is " My dear Friend."

Time; and yet, of the two, the latter is the most precious. I heartily wish you to be a good economist of both; and you are now of an age to begin to think seriously of these two important articles.
5 Young people are apt to think they have so much time before them, that they may squander what they please of it, and yet have enough left; as very great fortunes have frequently seduced people to a ruinous profusion. Fatal mistakes, always repented of, but
10 always too late! Old Mr. Lowndes, the famous Secretary of the Treasury, in the reigns of King William, Queen Anne, and King George the First, used to say, *Take care of the pence, and the pounds will take care of themselves.* To this maxim, which he not
15 only preached, but practiced, his two grandsons, at this time, owe the very considerable fortunes that he left them.

This holds equally true as to time; and I most earnestly recommend to you the care of those minutes
20 and quarters of hours, in the course of the day, which people think too short to deserve their attention; and yet, if summed up at the end of the year, would amount to a very considerable portion of time. For example; you are to be at such a place at twelve, by
25 appointment; you go out at eleven, to make two or three visits first; those persons are not at home: instead of sauntering away that intermediate time at a coffee-house, and possibly alone, return home, write a letter, beforehand, for the ensuing post, or take up a
30 good book, I do not mean Descartes, Mallebranche, Locke, or Newton, by way of dipping, but some book of rational amusement, and detached pieces, as

---

30 **Descartes, etc.** Four celebrated philosophers.

Horace, Boileau, Waller, La Bruyere, etc. This will
be so much time saved, and by no means ill employed.
Many people lose a great deal of time by reading;
for they read frivolous and idle books, such as the
absurd Romances of the two last centuries; where 5
characters, that never existed, are insipidly displayed,
and sentiments, that were never felt, pompously
described: the oriental ravings and extravagances of
the Arabian Nights, and Mogul Tales; or the new
flimsy *brochures* that now swarm in France, of Fairy 10
Tales, *Réflexions sur le Cœur et l'Esprit, Métaphysique
de l'Amour, Analyse des beaux Sentiments;* and such
sort of idle frivolous stuff, that nourishes and im-
proves the mind just as much as whipped cream
would the body. Stick to the best established books 15
in every language; the celebrated Poets, Historians,
Orators, or Philosophers. By these means (to use a
city metaphor) you will make fifty *per cent.* of that
time, of which others do not make above three or
four, or probably nothing at all.   20

Many people lose a great deal of their time by
laziness; they loll and yawn in a great chair, tell
themselves that they have not time to begin anything
then, and that it will do as well another time. This
is a most unfortunate disposition, and the greatest 25
obstruction to both knowledge and business. At
your age, you have no right nor claim to laziness;
I have, if I please, being *emeritus.* You are but just

¹ **Horace, etc.** Young Stanhope's scholarship seems to have been sufficient to
enable him to enjoy Latin and French authors in their original languages.

⁹ **Mogul Tales.** Mongolian Tales, similar to the better known Arabian Nights.

¹¹ **Reflexions . . . . Sentiments.** Reflections on the Heart and Spirit; The
Philosophy of Love ; Analysis of Fine Sentiment.

²⁸ **Emeritus.** Literally, *Having earned* (a rest). A title given to one honor-
ably retired from active duty.

listed in the world, and must be active, diligent, indefatigable. If ever you propose commanding with
dignity, you must serve up to it with diligence.
Never put off till to-morrow what you can do to-day.
5   Dispatch is the soul of business; and nothing con-
tributes more to Dispatch, than Method. Lay down
a method for everything, and stick to it inviolably,
as far as unexpected incidents may allow. Fix one
certain hour and day in the week for your accounts,
10 and keep them together in their proper order; by
which means they will require very little time, and you
can never be much cheated. Whatever letters and
papers you keep, docket and tie them up in their
respective classes, so that you may instantly have
15 recourse to any one. Lay down a method also for
your reading, for which you allot a certain share of
your mornings; let it be in a consistent and con-
secutive course, and not in that desultory and
immethodical manner, in which many people read
20 scraps of different authors, upon different subjects.
Keep a useful and short common-place book of what
you read, to help your memory only, and not for
pedantic quotations. Never read History without
having maps, and a chronological book, or tables,
25 lying by you, and constantly recurred to; without
which, History is only a confused heap of facts. One
method more I recommend to you, by which I have
found great benefit, even in the most dissipated part
of my life; that is, to rise early, and at the same hour
30 every morning, how late soever you may have sat
up the night before. This secures you an hour or
two, at least, of reading or reflection, before the
common interruptions of the morning begin; and it

will save your constitution, by forcing you to go to
bed early, at least one night in three.

You will say, it may be, as many young people
would, that all this order and method is very troublesome, only fit for dull people, and a disagreeable 5
restraint upon the noble spirit and fire of youth. I
deny it; and assert, on the contrary, that it will procure you both more time and more taste for your
pleasures; and so far from being troublesome to you,
that after you have pursued it a month it would be 10
troublesome to you to lay it aside. Business whets
the appetite, and gives a taste to pleasures, as exercise
does to food: and business can never be done without
method: it raises the spirits for pleasure; and a *specta-
cle*, a ball, an assembly, will much more sensibly affect 15
a man who has employed, than a man who has lost,
the preceding part of the day; nay, I will venture to
say, that a fine lady will seem to have more charms
to a man of study or business, than to a saunterer.
The same listlessness runs through his whole conduct, 20
and he is as insipid in his pleasures as inefficient in
everything else.

There is a certain dignity to be kept up in pleasures,
as well as in business. In love, a man may lose his
heart with dignity; but if he loses his nose, he loses 25
his character into the bargain. At table, a man may
with decency have a distinguishing palate; but indiscriminate voraciousness degrades him to a glutton.
A man may play with decency; but if he games, he
is disgraced. Vivacity and wit make a man shine in 30
company; but trite jokes and loud laughter reduce
him to a buffoon. Every virtue, they say, has its
kindred vice; every pleasure, I am sure, has its neigh-

listed in the world, and must be active, diligent, indefatigable. If ever you propose commanding with
dignity, you must serve up to it with diligence.
Never put off till to-morrow what you can do to-day.

    Dispatch is the soul of business; and nothing con-
tributes more to Dispatch, than Method. Lay down
a method for everything, and stick to it inviolably,
as far as unexpected incidents may allow. Fix one
certain hour and day in the week for your accounts,
and keep them together in their proper order; by
which means they will require very little time, and you
can never be much cheated. Whatever letters and
papers you keep, docket and tie them up in their
respective classes, so that you may instantly have
recourse to any one. Lay down a method also for
your reading, for which you allot a certain share of
your mornings; let it be in a consistent and con-
secutive course, and not in that desultory and
immethodical manner, in which many people read
scraps of different authors, upon different subjects.
Keep a useful and short common-place book of what
you read, to help your memory only, and not for
pedantic quotations. Never read History without
having maps, and a chronological book, or tables,
lying by you, and constantly recurred to; without
which, History is only a confused heap of facts. One
method more I recommend to you, by which I have
found great benefit, even in the most dissipated part
of my life; that is, to rise early, and at the same hour
every morning, how late soever you may have sat
up the night before. This secures you an hour or
two, at least, of reading or reflection, before the
common interruptions of the morning begin; and it

boring disgrace. Mark carefully, therefore, the line
that separates them, and rather stop a yard short, than
step an inch beyond it.

5 I wish to God that you had as much pleasure in
following my advice, as I have in giving it you; and
you may the easier have it, as I give you none that is
inconsistent with your pleasure. In all that I say to
you, it is your interest alone that I consider: trust to
my experience; you know you may to my affection.
10 Adieu.

Letter XXXII

VIRTUE: MODESTY

LONDON, May 17, O. S. 1750.

MY DEAR FRIEND: Your apprenticeship is near out,
and you are soon to set up for yourself; that approach-
ing moment is a critical one for you, and an anxious
15 one for me. A tradesman who would succeed in his
way must begin by establishing a character of integ-
rity and good manners: without the former, nobody
will go to his shop at all; without the latter, nobody
will go there twice. This rule does not exclude the
20 fair arts of trade. He may sell his goods at the best
price he can, within certain bounds. He may avail
himself of the humor, the whims, and the fantastical
tastes of his customers; but what he warrants to be
good must be really so, what he seriously asserts must
25 be true, or his first fraudulent profits will soon end
in a bankruptcy. It is the same in higher life and in
the great business of the world. A man who does
not solidly establish, and really deserve, a character

of truth, probity, good manners, and good morals at
his first setting out in the world, may impose and
shine like a meteor for a very short time, but will very
soon vanish, and be extinguished with contempt.
People easily pardon in young men the common 5
irregularities of the senses; but they do not forgive
the least vice of the heart. The heart never grows
better by age: I fear rather worse; always harder.
A young liar will be an old one, and a young knave
will only be a greater knave as he grows older. But 10
should a bad young heart, accompanied with a good
head (which by the way very seldom is the case), really
reform in a more advanced age, from a consciousness
of its folly, as well as of its guilt, such a conversion
would only be thought prudential and political, but 15
never sincere. I hope in God, and I verily believe
that you want no moral virtue. But the possession
of all the moral virtues *in actu primo*, as the logicians
call it, is not sufficient; you must have them *in actu
secundo* too; nay, that is not sufficient, neither, you 20
must have the reputation of them also. Your character in the world must be built upon that solid
foundation, or it will soon fall, and upon your own
head. You cannot therefore be too careful, too nice,
too scrupulous, in establishing this character at first, 25
upon which your whole career depends. Let no conversation, no example, no fashion, no *bon mot*, no
silly desire of seeming to be above what most knaves
and many fools call prejudices, ever tempt you to
avow, excuse, extenuate, or laugh at the least breach 30

---

18 **In actu primo.** In the first act.
19 **In actu secundo.** In the second act.
27 **Bon mot.** Witty remark.

of morality; but show upon all occasions, and take all occasions to show, a detestation and abhorrence of it. There, though young, you ought to be strict; and there only, while young, it becomes you to be 5 strict and severe. But there too, spare the persons while you lash the crimes. All this relates, as you easily judge, to the vices of the heart, such as lying, fraud, envy, malice, detraction, etc.

To come now to a point of much less but yet of 10 very great consequence at your first setting out. Be extremely on your guard against vanity, the common failing of inexperienced youth; but particularly against that kind of vanity that dubs a man a coxcomb,—a character which, once acquired, is more indelible than 15 that of the priesthood. It is not to be imagined by how many different ways vanity defeats its own purposes. Some men decide peremptorily upon every subject, betray their ignorance upon many, and show a disgusting presumption upon the rest. Others 20 flatter their vanity by little extraneous objects, which have not the least relation to themselves,—such as being descended from, related to, or acquainted with people of distinguished merit and eminent characters. They talk perpetually of their grandfather such-a-one, 25 their uncle such-a-one, and their intimate friend Mr. Such-a-one, with whom possibly they are hardly acquainted. But admitting it all to be as they would have it, what then? Have they the more merit for those accidents? Certainly not. On the contrary, 30 their taking up adventitious proves their want of intrinsic merit; a rich man never borrows. Take this rule for granted, as a never-failing one,—that you must never seem to affect the character in which you

have a mind to shine. Modesty is the only sure bait
when you angle for praise. The affectation of
courage will make even a brave man pass only for
a bully, as the affectation of wit will make a man of
parts pass for a coxcomb. By this modesty I do not 5
mean timidity and awkward bashfulness. On the
contrary, be inwardly firm and steady, know your own
value whatever it may be, and act upon that principle;
but take care to let nobody discover that you do know
your own value. Whatever real merit you have, 10
other people will discover, and people always magnify
their own discoveries, as they lessen those of others.

Letter XXXIII

IMPORTANCE OF GOOD ENUNCIATION

LONDON, July the 9th, O. S. 1750.
MY DEAR FRIEND: I should not deserve that appel-
lation in return from you, if I did not freely and 15
explicitly inform you of every corrigible defect, which
I may either hear of, suspect, or at any time discover
in you. Those who in the common course of the
world will call themselves your friends, or whom,
according to the common notions of friendship, you 20
may possibly think such, will never tell you of your
faults, still less of your weaknesses. But on the contrary, more desirous to make you their friend than
to prove themselves yours, they will flatter both, and,
in truth, not be sorry for either. Interiorly, most 25
people enjoy the inferiority of their best friends. The
useful and essential part of friendship to you is

reserved singly for Mr. Harte and myself; our relations to you stand pure, and unsuspected of all private
views.   In whatever we say to you, we can have no
interest but yours.   We can have no competition, no
5 jealousy, no secret envy or malignity.   We are therefore authorized to represent, advise, and remonstrate;
and your reason must tell you that you ought to attend
to and believe us.

I am credibly informed that there is still a con-
10 siderable hitch or hobble in your enunciation; and that
when you speak fast, you sometimes speak unin-
telligibly.   I have formerly and frequently laid my
thoughts before you so fully upon this subject, that
I can say nothing new upon it now.   I must there-
15 fore only repeat, that your whole depends upon it.
Your trade is to speak well, both in public and in
private.   The manner of your speaking is full as
important as the matter, as more people have ears
to be tickled than understandings to judge.   Be your
20 productions ever so good, they will be of no use, if
you stifle and strangle them in their birth.   The best
compositions of Corelli, if ill executed, and played
out of tune, instead of touching, as they do when well
performed, would only excite the indignation of the
25 hearers, when murdered by an unskillful performer.
But to murder your own productions, and that
coram populo, is a *Medean cruelty*, which Horace
absolutely forbids.   Remember of what importance
Demosthenes, and one of the Gracchi, thought *enun-*

---

22 **Corelli.** (1653–1713.) An Italian violinist and composer.

27 **Coram populo.** Publicly.

27 **Medean cruelty.** Medea is fabled to have murdered her own children.

29 **Gracchi.** The two best known Romans of this name were brothers, tribunes,

ciation; read what stress Cicero and Quintilian lay upon it; even the herb-women at Athens were correct judges of it. Oratory with all its graces, that of enunciation in particular, is full as necessary in our government, as it ever was in Greece or Rome. No 5 man can make a fortune or a figure in this country, without speaking, and speaking well, in public. If you will persuade, you must first please; and if you will please, you must tune your voice to harmony; you must articulate every syllable distinctly; your 10 emphasis and cadences must be strongly and properly marked; and the whole together must be graceful and engaging; if you do not speak in that manner, you had much better not speak at all. All the learning you have, or ever can have, is not worth one groat 15 without it. It may be a comfort and an amusement to you in your closet, but can be of no use to you in the world. Let me conjure you therefore to make this your only object, till you have absolutely conquered it, for that is in your power; think of nothing 20 else, read and speak for nothing else. Read aloud, though alone, and read articulately and distinctly, as if you were reading in public, and on the most important occasion. Recite pieces of eloquence, declaim scenes of tragedies, to Mr. Harte, as if he were 25 a numerous audience. If there is any particular consonant which you have a difficulty in articulating, as I think you had with the *R*, utter it millions and millions of times, till you have learned it right. Never speak quick, till you have first learned to speak well. 30

who lost their lives in endeavoring to check the avarice of the ruling party at Rome.

¹ Quintilian. (42?–118?) A noted Roman rhetorician and author.

In short, lay aside every book and every thought, that does not directly tend to this great object, absolutely decisive of your future fortune and figure.

The next thing necessary in your destination is, 5 writing correctly, elegantly, and in a good hand too; in which three particulars, I am sorry to tell you that you hitherto fail. Your handwriting is a very bad one, and would make a scurvy figure in an office-book of letters, or even in a lady's pocket-book. But 10 that fault is easily cured by care, since every man who has the use of his eyes and of his right hand can write whatever hand he pleases.

Letter XXXIV

HISTORY: CONVERSATION

LONDON, Nov. 1, O. S. 1750.

MY DEAR FRIEND: While you are in France, I 15 could wish that the hours you allot for historical amusement should be entirely devoted to the history of France. One always reads history to most advantage in that country to which it is relative,—not only books but persons being ever at hand to solve doubts 20 and clear up difficulties.

. . . .

Conversation in France, if you have the address and dexterity to turn it upon useful subjects, will exceeding improve your historical knowledge, for people there, however classically ignorant they may 25 be, think it a shame to be ignorant of the history of their own country; they read that, if they read nothing else, and having often read nothing else are proud of having read that, and talk of it willingly: even the women are well instructed in that sort of reading. I am far from meaning by this that you should always be talking wisely in company of books, history, and matters of knowledge. There are many companies which you will and ought to keep, where such con- 5 versations would be misplaced and ill-timed. Your own good sense must distinguish the company and the time. You must trifle only with triflers and be serious only with the serious, but dance to those who pipe. *"Cur in theatrum Cato severe venisti?"* was 10 justly said to an old man: how much more so would it be to one of your age! From the moment that you are dressed and go out, pocket all your knowledge with your watch, and never pull it out in company unless desired; the producing of the one unasked 15 implies that you are weary of the company, and the producing of the other unrequired will make the company weary of you. Company is a republic too jealous of its liberties to suffer a dictator even for a quarter of an hour, and yet in that, as in all republics, 20 there are some few who really govern; but then it is by seeming to disclaim, instead of attempting to usurp the power. That is the occasion in which manners, dexterity, address, and the undefinable *je ne sais quoi* triumph; if properly exerted their conquest is sure, 25 and the more lasting for not being perceived. Remember that this is not only your first and greatest, but ought to be almost your only object, while you are in France.

---

¹⁰ "Cur . . . . venisti?" "Cato, why do you come to the theater with such an austere countenance?"

²⁴ Je ne sais quoi. Literally that *I do not know what*, that indefinable something.

I know that many of your countrymen are apt to
call the freedom and vivacity of the French petulancy
and ill-breeding; but should you think so, I desire
upon many accounts that you will not say so. I
5 admit that it may be so in some instances of *petits
maîtres étourdis* and in some young people unbroken
to the world; but I can assure you that you will find
it much otherwise with people of a certain rank and
age, upon whose model you will do very well to form
10 yourself. We call their steady assurance, impudence.
Why? Only because what we call modesty is awkward bashfulness and *mauvaise honte*. For my part
I see no impudence, but on the contrary infinite utility
and advantage, in presenting one's self with the same
15 coolness and unconcern in any and every company;
till one can do that, I am very sure that one can never
present one's self well. Whatever is done under concern and embarrassment, must be ill done; and till
a man is absolutely easy and unconcerned in every
20 company he will never be thought to have kept good,
nor be very welcome in it. A steady assurance with
seeming modesty is possibly the most useful qualification that a man can have in every part of life. A man
would certainly not make a very considerable fortune
25 and figure in the world, whose modesty and timidity
should often, as bashfulness always does, put him in
the deplorable and lamentable situation of the pious
Æneas, when *obstupuit, steteruntque comæ, et vox fauci-
bus hæsit.* Fortune,

30   "——born to be controlled,
              Stoops to the forward and the bold."

ᵃ **Petits maitres étourdis.** Silly coxcombs.
²⁸ **Obstupuit . . . . hæsit.** Æneid, III. 774. "He was dumfounded,

Assurance and intrepidity, under the white banner of seeming modesty, clear the way for merit, that would otherwise be discouraged by difficulties in its journey; whereas barefaced impudence is the noisy and blustering harbinger of a worthless and sense- 5 less usurper.

You will think that I shall never have done recommending to you these exterior worldly accomplishments, and you will think right, for I never shall. They are of too great consequence to you for me to 10 be indifferent or negligent about them; the shining part of your future figure and fortune depends now wholly upon them. They are the acquisitions which must give efficacy and success to those you have already made. To have it said and believed that you 15 are the most learned man in England would be no more than was said and believed of Dr. Bentley; but to have it said at the same time that you are also the best bred, most polite, and agreeable man in the kingdom, would be such a happy composition of a char- 20 acter as I never yet knew any one man deserve, and which I endeavor as well as ardently wish that you may. Absolute perfection is, I well know, unattainable; but I know too that a man of parts may be unweariedly aiming at it, and arrive pretty near it. 25 Try, labor, persevere. Adieu.

---

his hair stood on end, and his voice stuck in his throat." (The original has the first verb in the first person).

[17] **Dr. Bentley.** (1662–1742.) The greatest classical scholar in England, who made enemies by his supercilious manner.

Letter XXXV

GOOD HANDWRITING

LONDON, Jan. the 28th, O. S. 1751.

MY DEAR FRIEND: A bill for ninety pounds sterling was brought me the other day, said to be drawn upon me by you; I scrupled paying it at first, not
5 upon account of the sum, but because you had sent me no letter of advice, which is always done in those transactions; and still more, because I did not perceive that you had signed it. The person who presented it desired me to look again, and that I should
10 discover your name at the bottom; accordingly I looked again, and with the help of my magnifying glass did perceive that what I had first taken only for somebody's mark was, in truth, your name, written in the worst and smallest hand I ever saw in my life.
15 However, I paid it at a venture; though I would almost rather lose the money, than that such a signature should be yours. All gentlemen, and all men of business, write their names always in the same way, that their signature may be so well
20 known as not to be easily counterfeited; and they generally sign in rather a larger character than their common hand; whereas your name was in a less, and a worse, than your common writing. This suggested to me the various accidents which
25 may very probably happen to you, while you write so ill. For instance; if you were to write in such a character to the secretary's office, your letter would immediately be sent to the decipherer, as containing

matters of the utmost secrecy, not fit to be trusted to the common character. If you were to write so to an antiquarian, he (knowing you to be a man of learning) would certainly try it by the Runic, Celtic, or Sclavonian alphabet, never suspecting it to be a 5 modern character.

I have often told you that every man who has the use of his eyes and of his hand can write whatever hand he pleases; and it is plain that you can, since you write both the Greek and German characters, 10 which you never learned of a writing-master, extremely well, though your common hand, which you learned of a master, is an exceeding bad and illiberal one, equally unfit for business or common use. I do not desire that you should write the labored, stiff 15 character of a writing-master: a man of business must write quick and well, and that depends singly upon use. I would therefore advise you to get some very good writing-master at Paris, and apply to it for a month only, which will be sufficient; for, upon my 20 word, the writing of a genteel plain hand of business is of much more importance than you think. You will say, it may be, that when you write so very ill, it is because you are in a hurry: to which I answer, Why are you ever in a hurry? a man of sense may be in 25 haste, but can never be in a hurry, because he knows, that whatever he does in a hurry he must necessarily do very ill. He may be in haste to dispatch an affair, but he will take care not to let that haste hinder his doing it well. Little minds are in a hurry, when the 30 object proves (as it commonly does) too big for them; they run, they hare, they puzzle, confound, and perplex themselves; they want to do everything at once,

and never do it at all. But a man of sense takes the
time necessary for doing the thing he is about, well;
and his haste to dispatch a business, only appears
by the continuity of his application to it: he pursues
5 it with a cool steadiness, and finishes it before he
begins any other. I own your time is much taken
up, and you have a great many different things to do;
but remember that you had much better do half of
them well, and leave the other half undone, than do
10 them all indifferently. Moreover, the few seconds
that are saved in the course of the day, by writing ill
instead of well, do not amount to an object of time,
by any means equivalent to the disgrace or ridicule of
writing a scrawl. Consider, that if your very bad
15 writing could furnish me with matter of ridicule, what
will it not do to others, who do not view you in that
partial light that I do. There was a Pope, I think it
was Pope Chigi, who was justly ridiculed for his
attention to little things, and his inability in great
20 ones; and therefore called *maximus in minimis*, and
minimus in maximis. Why? Because he attended
to little things, when he had great ones to do. At
this particular period of your life, and at the place you
are now in, you have only little things to do; and
25 you should make it habitual to you to do them well,
that they may require no attention from you when you
have, as I hope you will have, greater things to mind.
Make a good handwriting familiar to you now, that
you may hereafter have nothing but your matter to
30 think of, when you have occasion to write to Kings
and Ministers. Dance, dress, present yourself habitu-

---

20 Maximus . . . . in maximis. " In small things, the greatest ; in great
things, the least."

ally well now, that you may have none of those little things to think of hereafter, and which will be all necessary to be done well occasionally, when you will have greater things to do.

Letter XXXVI

ENGAGING MANNERS: "A RESPECTABLE HOTTENTOT"

LONDON, Feb. the 28th, O. S. 1751. 5
MY DEAR FRIEND: This epigram in Martial,

> " Non amo te, Sabidi, nec possum dicere quare,
> Hoc tantum possum dicere, non amo te ; "

has puzzled a great many people; who cannot conceive how it is possible not to love anybody, and yet 10 not to know the reason why. I think I conceive Martial's meaning very clearly, though the nature of epigram, which is to be short, would not allow him to explain it more fully; and I take it to be this: "O Sabidis, you are a very worthy deserving man; you 15 have a thousand good qualities, you have a great deal of learning: I esteem, I respect, but for the soul of me I cannot love, you, though I cannot particularly say why. You are not *aimable;* you have not those engaging manners, those pleasing attentions, those 20 graces, and that address, which are absolutely neces-

---

⁷ **Non amo te**, etc. Freely translated in lines 14, etc. The familiar English version originated as follows: T. Brown (1663-1704) while a student at Christ Church, Oxford, being in disgrace, was set by Dr. Fell, the Dean of the College, to translate this epigram of Martial. He rendered it thus:

> "I do not love thee, Doctor Fell,
> The reason why I cannot tell ;
> But this alone I know full well,
> I do not love thee, Doctor Fell."

¹⁹ **Aimable.** Amiable.

sary to please, though impossible to define. I cannot
say it is this or that particular thing that hinders me
from loving you, it is the whole together; and upon
the whole you are not agreeable." How often have
5 I, in the course of my life, found myself in this situation, with regard to many of my acquaintance, whom
I have honored and respected, without being able to
love! I did not know why, because, when one is
young, one does not take the trouble, nor allow one's
10 self the time, to analyze one's sentiments, and to trace
them up to their source. But subsequent observation and reflection have taught me why.

There is a man, whose moral character, deep learning, and superior parts, I acknowledge, admire, and
15 respect; but whom it is so impossible for me to love,
that I am almost in a fever whenever I am in his company. His figure (without being deformed) seems
made to disgrace or ridicule the common structure of
the human body. His legs and arms are never in the
20 position which, according to the situation of his body,
they ought to be in; but constantly employed in com-
mitting acts of hostility upon the graces. He throws
anywhere, but down his throat, whatever he means to
drink; and only mangles what he means to carve.
25 Inattentive to all the regards of social life, he mis-
times or misplaces everything. He disputes with
heat, and indiscriminately; mindless of the rank,
character, and situation of those with whom he disputes: absolutely ignorant of the several gradations
30 of familiarity or respect, he is exactly the same to his
superiors, his equals, and his inferiors; and therefore,
by a necessary consequence, absurd to two of the
three. Is it possible to love such a man? No. The

utmost I can do for him, is to consider him as a respectable Hottentot.

Letter XXXVII

" SUAVITER IN MODO, FORTITER IN RE "

MY DEAR FRIEND: I mentioned to you some time ago, a sentence, which I would most earnestly wish you always to retain in your thoughts and observe in your conduct. It is *Suaviter in modo, fortiter in re.* I do not know any one rule so unexceptionally useful and necessary in every part of life. I shall therefore take it for my text to-day; and as old men love preaching, and I have some right to preach to you, I here present you with my sermon upon these words. To proceed then regularly and *pulpitically*, I will first show you, my beloved, the necessary connection of the two members of my text,—*Suaviter in modo: fortiter in re.* In the next place, I shall set forth the advantages and utility resulting from a strict observance of the precept contained in my text; and conclude with an application of the whole. The *suaviter in modo* alone would degenerate and sink into a mean, timid complaisance and passiveness, if not supported and dignified by the *fortiter in re,* which would also run

---

² **A respectable Hottentot.** This is supposed to refer to Dr. Samuel Johnson, whose manners, especially at table, must have been extremely repugnant to Lord Chesterfield's sensibilities. See Macaulay's Essay on Johnson, Maynard's English Classic Series, No. 178.

⁶ **Suaviter in modo, fortiter in re.** "Suave in manner, firm in act." "An iron hand in a velvet glove."

¹² **Pulpitically.** After the manner of the pulpit. Observe how, throughout the letter, he imitates the style of a preacher.

into impetuosity and brutality, if not tempered and
softened by the *suaviter in modo:* however, they are
seldom united.   The warm, choleric man with strong
animal spirits despises the *suaviter in modo*, and thinks
5 to carry all before him by the *fortiter in re*.   He may
possibly, by great accident, now and then succeed,
when he has only weak and timid people to deal with;
but his general fate will be to shock, offend, be hated,
and fail.   On the other hand, the cunning, crafty man
10 thinks to gain all his ends by the *suaviter in modo*
only; *he becomes all things to all men;* he seems to
have no opinion of his own, and servilely adopts the
present opinion of the present person; he insinuates
himself only into the esteem of fools, but is soon de-
15 tected, and surely despised by everybody else.   The
wise man (who differs as much from the cunning as
from the choleric man) alone joins the *suaviter in
modo* with the *fortiter in re*.   Now to the advantages
arising from the strict observance of this precept.   If
20 you are in authority and have a right to command,
your commands delivered *suaviter in modo* will be
willingly, cheerfully, and consequently well obeyed;
whereas, if given only *fortiter*, that is brutally, they
will rather, as Tacitus says, be interrupted than exe-
25 cuted.   For my own part, if I bid my footman bring
me a glass of wine in a rough, insulting manner, I
should expect that in obeying me he would contrive
to spill some of it upon me, and I am sure I should
deserve it.   A cool, steady resolution should show
30 you that where you have a right to command you will
be obeyed, but at the same time a gentleness in the
manner of enforcing that obedience could make it a

---

11 **All things to all men.   A perversion of St. Paul's advice to Timothy.**

cheerful one, and soften as much as possible the
mortifying consciousness of inferiority. If you are to
ask a favor or even to solicit your due you must do it
suaviter in modo or you will give those who have a
mind to refuse you either, a pretense to do it by resent- 5
ing the manner; but on the other hand you must by
a steady perseverance and decent tenaciousness show
the *fortiter in re.* The right motives are seldom the
true ones of men's actions, especially of kings, ministers, and people in high stations, who often give to 10
importunity and fear what they would refuse to
justice or to merit. By the *suaviter in modo* engage
their hearts if you can: at least prevent the pretense
of offense: but take care to show enough of the
fortiter in re to extort from their love of ease or their 15
fear what you might in vain hope for from their justice or good nature. People in high life are har-
dened to the wants and distresses of mankind as
surgeons are to their bodily pains; they see and hear
of them all day long, and even of so many simulated 20
ones that they do not know which are real and which
are not. Other sentiments are therefore to be ap-
plied to than those of mere justice and humanity.
Their favor must be captivated by the *suaviter in
modo;* their love of ease disturbed by unwearied 25
importunity; or their fears wrought upon by a decent
intimation of implacable cool resentment,—this is
the true *fortiter in re.* This precept is the only way
I know in the world of being loved without being
despised, and feared without being hated. It consti- 30
tutes the dignity of character which every wise man
must endeavor to establish.

---

³¹ **Dignity of character.** This should be dignity of *manner*, which may be

Now to apply what has been said, and so conclude.

If you find that you have a hastiness in your temper which unguardedly breaks out into indiscreet
5 sallies or rough expressions to either your superiors, your equals, or your inferiors, watch it narrowly, check it carefully, and call the *suaviter in modo* to your assistance; at the first impulse of passion, be silent till you can be soft. Labor even to get the command
10 of your countenance so well that those emotions may not be read in it,—a most unspeakable advantage in business. On the other hand, let no complaisance, no gentleness of temper, no weak desire of pleasing on your part, no wheedling, coaxing, nor flattery on
15 other people's, make you recede one jot from any point that reason and prudence have bid you pursue; but return to the charge, persist, persevere, and you will find most things attainable that are possible. A yielding, timid meekness is always abused and in-
20 sulted by the unjust and the unfeeling; but when sustained by the *fortiter in re* is always respected, commonly successful. In your friendships and connections, as well as in your enmities, this rule is particularly useful: let your firmness and vigor preserve
25 and invite attachments to you, but at the same time let your manner hinder the enemies of your friends and dependents from becoming yours; let your enemies be disarmed by the gentleness of your manner, but let them feel at the same time the steadiness of
30 your just resentment,—for there is a great difference between bearing malice, which is always ungenerous,

---

the outward manifestation of dignity of character. Lord Chesterfield is prone to
emphasize externals to the neglect of true nobility of soul.

and a resolute self-defense, which is always prudent and justifiable.

. . . .

Some people cannot gain upon themselves to be easy and civil to those who are either their rivals, competitors, or opposers, though, independently of 5 these accidental circumstances, they would like and esteem them. They betray a shyness and an awkwardness in company with them, and catch at any little thing to expose them, and so from temporary and only occasional opponents make them their per- 10 sonal enemies. This is exceedingly weak and detrimental, as indeed is all humor in business, which can only be carried on successfully by unadulterated good policy and right reasoning. In such situations I would be more particularly and *noblement* civil, easy, 15 and frank with the man whose designs I traversed. This is commonly called generosity and magnanimity, but is in truth good sense and policy. The manner is often as important as the matter, sometimes more so. A favor may make an enemy and an injury may make 20 a friend, according to the different manner in which they are severally done. The countenance, the address, the words, the enunciation, the Graces add great efficacy to the *suaviter in modo* and great dignity to the *fortiter in re;* and consequently they de- 25 serve the utmost attention.

From what has been said, I conclude with this observation,—that gentleness of manners with firmness of mind is a short but full description of human perfection on this side of religious and moral duties. 30

---

13 **Humor.** Ill temper.
15 **Noblement.** Nobly.

That you may be seriously convinced of this truth
and show it in your life and conversation, is the most
sincere and ardent wish of   Yours.

Letter XXXVIII

BUSINESS HABITS

LONDON, Dec. the 19th, O. S. 1751.
5 MY DEAR FRIEND: You are now entered upon a
scene of business, where I hope you will one day
make a figure. Use does a great deal, but care and
attention must be joined to it. The first thing necessary in writing letters of business, is extreme clear-
10 ness and perspicuity; every paragraph should be so
clear, and unambiguous, that the dullest fellow in the
world may not be able to mistake it, nor obliged to
read it twice in order to understand it. This necessary clearness implies a correctness, without exclud-
15 ing an elegancy of style. Tropes, figures, antitheses,
epigrams, etc., would be as misplaced, and as impertinent, in letters of business, as they are sometimes (if
judiciously used) proper and pleasing in familiar
letters, upon common and trite subjects. In busi-
20 ness, an elegant simplicity, the result of care, not of
labor, is required. Business must be well, not
affectedly, dressed, but by no means negligently. Let
your first attention be to clearness, and read every
paragraph after you have written it, in the critical
25 view of discovering whether it is possible that any
one man can mistake the true sense of it; and correct
it accordingly.
Our pronouns and relatives often create obscurity

or ambiguity; be therefore exceedingly attentive to them, and take care to mark out with precision their particular relations. For example; Mr. Johnson acquainted me, that he had seen Mr. Smith, who had promised him to speak to Mr. Clarke, to return him 5 (Mr. Johnson) those papers, which he (Mr. Smith) had left some time ago with him (Mr. Clarke): it is better to repeat a name, though unnecessarily, ten times, than to have the person mistaken once.

Business does not exclude (as possibly you wish it 10 did) the usual terms of politeness and good breeding; but, on the contrary, strictly requires them: such as, *I have the honor to acquaint your Lordship; Permit me to assure you; If I may be allowed to give my opinion, etc.* For the Minister abroad, who writes to the Min- 15 ister at home, writes to his superior; possibly to his patron, or at least to one who he desires should be so.

Letters of business will not only admit of, but be the better for, *certain graces:* but then they must be scattered with a sparing and a skillful hand; they 20 must fit their place exactly. They must decently adorn without encumbering, and modestly shine without glaring. But as this is the utmost degree of perfection in letters of business, I would not advise you to attempt those embellishments till you have first 25 laid your foundation well.

But (I repeat it again) there is an elegant simplicity and dignity of style absolutely necessary for good letters of business; attend to that carefully. Let your periods be harmonious, without seeming to be 30 labored; and let them not be too long, for that always occasions a degree of obscurity. I should not mention correct orthography, but that you very often fail

in that particular, which will bring ridicule upon you;
for no man is allowed to spell ill. I wish, too, that
your handwriting were much better: and I cannot
conceive why it is not, since every man may certainly
5 write whatever hand he pleases. Neatness in folding
up, sealing, and directing your packets, is by no
means to be neglected, though I dare say you think
it is. But there is something in the exterior, even of
a packet, that may please or displease; and conse-
10 quently worth some attention.

You say that your time is very well employed, and
so it is, though as yet only in the outlines and first
routine of business. They are previously necessary to
be known; they smooth the way for parts and dex-
15 terity. Business requires no conjuration nor super-
natural talents, as people unacquainted with it are apt
to think. Method, diligence, and discretion will carry
a man of good strong common sense much higher
than the finest parts without them can do. *Par*
20 *negotiis, neque supra*, is the true character of a man
of business: but then it implies ready attention, and
no *absences;* and a flexibility and versatility of attention from one object to another, without being engrossed by any one.

25 Be upon your guard against the pedantry and
affectation of business, which young people are apt
to fall into from the pride of being concerned in it
young. They look thoughtful, complain of the
weight of business, throw out mysterious hints, and
30 seem big with secrets which they do not know. Do
you, on the contrary, never talk of business, but to

---

[19] Par negotiis, neque supra. *Tacitus.* " Neither above nor below his
business."

those with whom you are to transact it; and learn to seem *vacuus*, and idle, when you have the most business. Of all things the *volto sciolto*, and the *pensieri stretti*, are necessary. Adieu.

Letter XXXIX

READING HISTORY

LONDON, February the 14th, O. S. 1752. 5
MY DEAR FRIEND: In a month's time, I believe, I shall have the pleasure of sending you, and you will have the pleasure of reading, a work of Lord Bolingbroke's in two volumes octavo, *Upon the Use of History;* in several Letters to Lord Hyde, then Lord 10 Cornbury. It is now put into the press. It is hard to determine whether this work will instruct or please most: the most material historical facts, from the great era of the treaty of Münster, are touched upon, accompanied by the most solid reflections, and 15 adorned by all that elegancy of style, which was peculiar to himself, and in which, if Cicero equals, he certainly does not exceed him; but every other writer

---

² **Vacuus.** Empty.

³ **Volto sciolto.** Open countenance. *Il volto sciolto et i pensieri stretti* is an Italian proverb : *Preserve an open countenance, but conceal your thoughts.*

⁸ **Lord Bolingbroke's.** Henry St. John, Viscount Bolingbroke. (1678–1751.) A handsome, brilliant, eloquent, licentious, and unprincipled politician. "Lord Bolingbroke," said Aaron Hill, "was the finest gentleman I ever saw." "To make St. John more polite," was a synonym for an impossibility. He was a master of English style, and has been called "the Cicero of our tongue." Pitt said "I would rather have a speech of Bolingbroke's than any of the lost treasures of antiquity."

¹⁴ **Treaty of Münster.** The treaty of Münster (or Westphalia), October 24, 1648, closed the Thirty Years' War, and became the basis of European international law.

falls short of him.   I would advise you almost to get
this book by heart.   I think you have a turn to history, you love it, and have a memory to retain it;
this book will teach you the proper use of it.   Some
5 people load their memories, indiscriminately, with
historical facts, as others do their stomachs with food;
and bring out the one, and bring up the other, entirely
crude and undigested.   You will find in Lord Bolingbroke's book, an infallible specific against that
10 epidemical complaint.

I remember a gentleman, who had read History in
this thoughtless and undistinguishing manner, and
who, having traveled, had gone through the Valteline.   He told me that it was a miserable, poor coun-
15 try, and therefore it was, surely, a great error in
Cardinal Richelieu, to make such a rout, and put
France to so much expense about it.   Had my friend
read History as he ought to have done, he would
have known that the great object of that great Minis-
20 ter was to reduce the power of the house of Austria;
and, in order to that, to cut off as much as he could
the communication between the several parts of their
extensive dominions; which reflections would have
justified the Cardinal to him in the affair of the
25 Valteline.   But it was easier to him to remember
facts, than to combine and reflect.

---

13 **Valteline.**   The upper valley of the Adda, in the extreme north of Italy.
Spelled, also, *Valtelline* and *Valtellina.*

16 **Cardinal Richelieu.**   (1585-1642.)   An able French statesman, prime minister of Louis XIII., and virtual ruler of France from 1624 till his death.

Letter XL

AIM AT PERFECTION

· LONDON, Feby. 20, O. S. 1752.

MY DEAR FRIEND: In all systems whatever, whether of religion, government, morals, etc., perfection is the object always proposed, though possibly unattainable,—hitherto at least certainly 5 unattained. However, those who aim carefully at the mark itself will unquestionably come nearer to it than those who from despair, negligence, or indolence leave to chance the work of skill. This maxim holds equally true in common life; those who aim at per- 10 fection will come infinitely nearer it than those desponding or indolent spirits who foolishly say to themselves, "Nobody is perfect; perfection is unattainable; to attempt it is chimerical; I shall do as well as others; why then should I give myself trouble 15 to be what I never can, and what according to the common course of things I need not be,—*perfect?*"

I am very sure that I need not point out to you the weakness and the folly of this reasoning. It would discourage and put a stop to the exertion of any one 20 of our faculties. On the contrary, a man of sense and spirit says to himself, "Though the point of perfection may (considering the imperfection of our nature) be unattainable, my care, my endeavors, my attention, shall not be wanting to get as near to it as 25 I can. I will approach it every day: possibly I may arrive at it at last; at least—what I am sure is in my own power—I will not be distanced." Many fools

(speaking of you) say to me, "What! would you
have him perfect?" I answer, Why not? What
hurt would it do to him or me? "Oh, but that is
impossible," say they; I reply, I am not sure of that:
5 perfection in the abstract I admit to be unattainable,
but what is commonly called perfection in a character, I maintain to be attainable, and not only that, but
in every man's power. "He has," continue they, "a
good head, a good heart, a good fund of knowledge,
10 which would increase daily: what would you have
more?" Why, I would have everything more that
can adorn and complete a character. Will it do his
head, his heart, or his knowledge any harm to have
the utmost delicacy of manners, the most shining
15 advantages of air and address, the most endearing
attentions and the most engaging graces? "But as
he is," say they, "he is loved wherever he is known."
I am very glad of it, say I: but I would have him be
liked before he is known and loved afterward. I
20 would have him by his first *abord* and address, make
people wish to know him, and inclined to love him;
he will save a great deal of time by it. "Indeed,"
reply they, "you are too nice, too exact, and lay too
much stress upon things that are of very little conse-
25 quence." Indeed, rejoin I, you know very little of
the nature of mankind, if you take these things to be
of little consequence; one cannot be too attentive to
them; it is they that always engage the heart, of which
the understanding is commonly the bubble. And I
30 would much rather that he erred in a point of gram-
mar, of history, of philosophy, etc., than in point of
manners and address. "But consider, he is very
young: all this will come in time." I hope so; but

that time must be when he is young, or it will never be at all; the right *pli* must be taken young, or it will never be easy or seem natural. "Come, come," say they (substituting as is frequently done, assertion instead of argument), "depend upon it, he will do 5 very well; and you have a great deal of reason to be satisfied with him." I hope and believe he will do well, but I would have him do better than well. I am very well pleased with him, but I would be more,—I would be proud of him. I would have him 10 have luster as well as weight. "Did you ever know anybody that re-united all these talents?" Yes, I did: Lord Bolingbroke joined all the politeness, the manners, and the graces of a courtier to the solidity of a statesman and to the learning of a pedant. He 15 was *omnis homo;* and pray what should hinder my boy from being so too, if he has, as I think he has, all the other qualifications that you allow him? Nothing can hinder him but neglect of or inattention to those objects which his own good sense must tell 20 him are of infinite consequence to him, and which therefore I will not suppose him capable of either neglecting or despising.

This (to tell you the whole truth) is the result of a controversy that passed yesterday between Lady 25 Hervy and myself, upon your subject and almost in the very words. I submit the decision of it to yourself; let your own good sense determine it, and make you act in consequence of that determination. The receipt to make this composition is short and infal- 30 lible; here I give it you:—

---

² Pli. Bent, direction.

¹⁶ Omnis homo. "A man symmetrically developed in every faculty."

Take variety of the best company wherever you are;
be minutely attentive to every word and action; imitate respectively those whom you observe to be
distinguished and considered for any one accomplish-
5 ment; then mix all those several accomplishments
together and serve them up yourself to others.

. . . .

Letter XLI

HEALTH: TIME: IDLENESS

LONDON, March the 5th, O. S. 1752.
MY DEAR FRIEND: As I have received no letter
from you by the usual post, I am uneasy upon account
10 of your health; for, had you been well, I am sure you
would have written, according to your engagement,
and my requisition. You have not the least notion
of any care of your health: but, though I would not
have you be a valetudinarian, I must tell you, that the
15 best and most robust health requires some degree of
attention to preserve. Young fellows, thinking they
have so much health and time before them, are very
apt to neglect or lavish both, and beggar themselves
before they are aware: whereas a prudent economy
20 in both, would make them rich indeed; and so far
from breaking in upon their pleasures, would improve
and almost perpetuate them. Be you wiser; and, before it is too late, manage both with care and fru-
gality; and lay out neither, but upon good interest
25 and security.
I will now confine myself to the employment of
your time, which, though I have often touched upon

formerly, is a subject that, from its importance, will bear repetition. You have, it is true, a great deal of time before you; but, in this period of your life, one hour usefully employed may be worth more than four-and-twenty hereafter; a minute is precious to 5 you now, whole days may possibly not be so forty years hence. Whatever time you allow or can snatch for serious reading (I say snatch, because company. and the knowledge of the world, is now your chief object), employ it in the reading of some one book, 10 and that a good one, till you have finished it: and do not distract your mind with various matters at the same time. In this light I would recommend to you to read *tout de suite* Grotius *de Jure Belli et Pacis*, translated by Barbeyrac, and Puffendorf's *Jus Gen-* 15 *tium*, translated by the same hand. For accidental quarters of hours, read works of invention, wit, and humor, of the best, and not of trivial, authors, either ancient or modern.

Whatever business you have, do it the first moment 20 you can; never by halves, but finish it without inter- ruption, if possible. Business must not be sauntered and trifled with; and you must not say to it, as Felix did to Paul, " at a more convenient season I will speak to thee." The most convenient season for business 25 is the first; but study and business, in some measure, point out their own times to a man of sense; time is much oftener squandered away in the wrong choice and improper methods of amusement and pleasures.

Many people think that they are in pleasures, pro- 30

---

[14] Tout de suite. Immediately.
[14] De Jure Belli et Pacis. On the Law of War and Peace.
[15] Jus Gentium. The Law of Nations.

vided they are neither in study nor in business.
Nothing like it; they are doing nothing, and might
just as well be asleep. They contract habitudes
from laziness, and they only frequent those places
5 where they are free from all restraints and attentions.
Be upon your guard against this idle profusion of
time: and let every place you go to be either the
scene of quick and lively pleasures, or the school
of your improvements: let every company you go
10 into, either gratify your senses, extend your knowledge, or refine your manners.   Have some decent
object of gallantry in view at some places; frequent
others, where people of wit and taste assemble; get
into others, where people of superior rank and dignity
15 command respect and attention from the rest of the
company; but pray frequent no neutral places, from
mere idleness and indolence.   Nothing forms a young
man so much as being used to keep respectable and
superior company, where a constant regard and atten-
20 tion is necessary.   It is true, this is at first a disagreeable state of restraint; but it soon grows
habitual, and consequently easy; and you are amply
paid for it, by the improvement you make, and the
credit it gives you.
25   Sloth, indolence, and *mollesse* are pernicious and
unbecoming a young fellow; let them be your *ressource* forty years hence at soonest.   Determine, at
all events and however disagreeable it may be to you
in some respects, and for some time, to keep the most
30 distinguished and fashionable company of the place
you are at, either for their rank, or for their learning,

---

25 Mollesse. Softness, effeminacy.
26 Ressource. Resource.

or *le bel esprit et le goût*. This gives you credentials
to the best companies,. wherever you go afterward.
Pray, therefore, no idolence, no laziness; but employ
every minute of your life in active pleasures or useful
employments. Address yourself to some woman of 5
fashion and beauty, wherever you are, and try how
far that will go. If the place be not secured beforehand, and garrisoned, nine times in ten you will take
it. By attentions and respect, you may always get
into the highest company; and by some admiration 10
and applause, whether merited or not, you may be
sure of being welcome among *les savants et les beaux
esprits*. There are but these three sorts of company
for a young fellow; there being neither pleasure nor
profit in any other. 15

Letter XLII

AVOIR DU MONDE

LONDON, April the 30th, O..S. 1752.
MY DEAR FRIEND: *Avoir du monde* is, in my
opinion, a very just and happy expression, for having address, manners, and for knowing how to behave
properly in all companies; and it implies, very truly, 20
that a man that hath not these accomplishments is
not of the world. Without them, the best parts are
inefficient, civility is absurd, and freedom offensive.
A learned parson, rusting in his cell at Oxford or
Cambridge, will reason admirably well upon the 25
nature of man; will profoundly analyze the head, the

---

[1] **Le bel esprit, etc.** Wit and style.
[13] **Les savants, etc.** The wise and the witty.
[17] **Avoir du monde.** To have a knowledge of the world.

heart, the reason, the will, the passions, the senses,
the sentiments, and all those subdivisions of we know
not what; and yet, unfortunately, he knows nothing
of man: for he hath not lived with him; and is igno-
5 rant of all the various modes, habits, prejudices, and
tastes, that always influence, and often determine him.
He views man as he does colors in Sir Isaac Newton's
prism, where only the capital ones are seen; but an
experienced dyer knows all their various shades and
10 gradations, together with the result of their several
mixtures.   Few men are of one plain, decided color;
most are mixed, shaded, and blended; and vary as
much, from different situations, as changeable silks
do from different lights.   The man *qui a du monde*
15 knows all this from his own experience and observation: the conceited, cloistered philosopher knows
nothing of it from his own theory; his practice is
absurd and improper; and he acts as awkwardly as a
man would dance, who has never seen others dance,
20 nor learned of a dancing-master; but who had only
studied the notes by which dances are now pricked
down, as well as tunes.   Observe and imitate, then,
the address, the arts, and the manners of those *qui
ont du monde:* see by what methods they first make,
25 and afterward improve, impressions in their favor.
Those impressions are much oftener owing to little
causes, than to intrinsic merit; which is less volatile,
and hath not so sudden an effect. Strong minds have
undoubtedly an ascendant over weak ones, as Galigai
30 Maréchale d'Ancre very justly observed, when to the

---

14 Qui a du monde. Who has this knowledge of the world.
23 Qui ont, etc. Who have, etc.
29 Galigai. Leonora Galigai, wife of Concini, Marshal Ancre, was executed
as a sorceress in 1617.

disgrace and reproach of those times, she was executed for having governed Mary of Medicis by the
arts of witchcraft and magic. But the ascendant is
to be gained by degrees, and by those arts only which
experience and the knowledge of the world teaches: 5
for few are mean enough to be bullied, though most
are weak enough to be bubbled. I have often seen
people of superior governed by people of much
inferior parts, without knowing or even suspecting
that they were so governed. This can only happen, 10
when those people of inferior parts have more worldly
dexterity and experience than those they govern.
They see the weak and unguarded part, and apply to
it: they take it, and all the rest follows. Would you
gain either men or women, and every man of sense 15
desires to gain both, *il faut du monde*. You have had
more opportunities than ever any man had, at your
age, of acquiring *ce monde;* you have been in the
best companies of most countries, at an age when
others have hardly been in any company at all. You 20
are master of all those languages, which John Trott
seldom speaks at all, and never well; consequently
you need be a stranger nowhere. This is the way,
and the only way, of having *du monde;* but if you
have it not, and have still any coarse rusticity about 25
you, may one not apply to you the *rusticus expectat*
of Horace?

---

² **Mary of Medicis.** Wife of Henry IV. of France, mother of Louis XIII., and
queen regent of France from the assassination of Henry IV. in 1610 to the accession
of Louis XIII. in 1614.

¹⁶ **Il faut du monde.** You must know the world.

¹⁸ **Ce monde.** This (knowledge of the) world.

²¹ **John Trott.** The average Englishman.

²⁶ **Rusticus expectat, dum defluat amnis.** Horace, Epistles, I. 2, 42. "The
countryman waits for the river to run dry."

This knowledge of the world teaches us more particularly two things, both which are of infinite consequence, and to neither of which nature inclines us; I mean, the command of ur temper and of our
5 countenance. A man who has no *monde* is inflamed with anger, or annihilated with shame, at every disagreeable incident: the one makes him act and talk like a madman, the other makes him look like a fool. But a man who has *du monde* seems not to understand
10 what he cannot or ought not to resent. If he makes a slip himself, he recovers it by his coolness, instead of plunging deeper by his confusion, like a stumbling horse. He is firm, but gentle; and practices that most excellent maxim, *suaviter in modo, fortiter in re.*
15 The other is the *volto sciolto e pensieri stretti.* People unused to the world have babbling countenances; and are unskillful enough to show what they have sense enough not to tell. In the course of the world, a man must very often put on an easy, frank counte-
20 nance upon very disagreeable occasions; he must seem pleased when he is very much otherwise; he must be able to accost, and receive with smiles, those whom he would much rather meet with swords. In Courts he must not turn himself inside out. All this
25 may, nay must, be done without falsehood and treachery: for it must go no further than politeness and manners, and must stop short of assurances and professions of simulated friendship. Good manners, to those one does not love, are no more a breach of
30 truth than " your humble servant " at the bottom of a challenge is; they are universally agreed upon, and understood, to be things of course. They are necessary guards of the decency and peace of society: they

must only act defensively; and then not with arms
poisoned with perfidy. Truth, but not the whole
truth, must be the invariable principle of every man,
who hath either religion, honor, or prudence. Those
who violate it may be cunning, but they are not able. 5
Lies and perfidy are the refuge of fools and cowards.
Adieu!

Letter XLIII

CIVILITY

LONDON, May the 11th, O. S. 1752.

MY DEAR FRIEND: I break my word by writing this
letter; but I break it on the allowable side, by doing 10
more than I promised. I have pleasure in writing to
you; and you may possibly have some profit in reading what I write; either of the motives were sufficient
for me, both I cannot withstand.

Another thing, which I most earnestly recommend 15
to you, not only in Germany, but in every part of
the world, where you may ever be, is, not only real,
but seeming attention, to whomever you speak to,
or to whoever speaks to you. There is nothing so
brutally shocking, nor so little forgiven, as a seeming 20
inattention to the person who is speaking to you;
and I have known many a man knocked down, for
(in my opinion) a much slighter provocation, than
that shocking inattention which I mean. I have seen
many people, who while you are speaking to them, 25
instead of looking at, and attending to, you, fix their
eyes upon the ceiling, or some other part of the
room, look out of the window, play with a dog, twirl
their snuff-box, or pick their nose. Nothing dis-

covers a little, futile, frivolous mind more than this, and nothing is so offensively ill-bred: it is an explicit declaration on your part, that every, the most trifling object, deserves your attention more than all that 5 can be said by the person who is speaking to you. Judge of the sentiments of hatred and resentment, which such treatment must excite, in every breast where any degree of self-love dwells; and I am sure I never yet met with that breast where there was not 10 a great deal. I repeat it again and again (for it is highly necessary for you to remember it), that sort of vanity and self-love is inseparable from human nature, whatever may be its rank or condition; even your footman will sooner forget and forgive a beating 15 than any manifest mark of slight and contempt. Be therefore, I beg of you, not only really, but seemingly and manifestly, attentive to whoever speaks to you; nay more, take their tone, and tune yourself to their unison. Be serious with the serious, gay with 20 the gay, and trifle with the triflers. In assuming these various shapes, endeavor to make each of them seem to sit easy upon you, and even to appear to be your own natural one. This is the true and useful versatility of which a thorough knowledge of the 25 world at once teaches the utility, and the means of acquiring.

I am very sure, at least I hope, that you will never make use of a silly expression, which is the favorite expression, and the absurd excuse of all fools and 30 blockheads; *I cannot do such a thing:* a thing by no means either morally or physically impossible. I *cannot* attend long together to the same thing, says one fool: that is, he is such a fool that he will not.

I remember a very awkward fellow, who did not know what to do with his sword, and who always took it off before dinner, saying, that he could not possibly dine with his sword on; upon which I could not help telling him that I really believed he could, without 5 any probable danger either to himself or others. It is a shame and an absurdity, for any man to say, that he cannot do all those things which are commonly done by all the rest of mankind.

Another thing, that I must earnestly warn you 10 against, is laziness; by which more people have lost the fruit of their travels, than (perhaps) by any other thing. Pray be always in motion. Early in the morning go and see things; and the rest of the day go and see people. If you stay but a week at a place, 15 and that an insignificant one, see, however, all that is to be seen there; know as many people, and get into as many houses, as ever you can.

I recommend to you likewise, though probably you have thought of it yourself, to carry in your pocket 20 a map of Germany, in which the post roads are marked; and also some short book of travels through Germany. The former will help to imprint in your memory situations and distances; and the latter will point out many things for you to see, that might 25 otherwise possibly escape you; and which, though they may in themselves be of little consequence, you would regret not having seen, after having been at the places where they were.

Thus warned and provided for your journey, God 30 speed you; *Felix faustumque sit!* Adieu.

---

²¹ **Felix faustumque sit.** " May it [the journey] be pleasant and propitious."

Letter XLIV

KNOWLEDGE OF BOOKS: IGNORANCE OF MEN

LONDON, May the 27th, O. S. 1753.

MY DEAR FRIEND: I have this day been tired, jaded, nay, tormented, by the company of a most worthy, sensible, and learned man, a near relation of
5 mine, who dined and passed the evening with me. This seems a paradox, but it is a plain truth; he has no knowledge of the world, no manners, no address; far from talking without book, as is commonly said of people who talk sillily, he only talks by book; which,
10 in general conversation, is ten times worse. He has formed in his own closet, from books, certain systems of everything, argues tenaciously upon those principles, and is both surprised and angry at whatever deviates from them. His theories are good, but,
15 unfortunately, are all impractical. Why? Because he has only read, and not conversed. He is acquainted with books, and an absolute stranger to men. Laboring with his matter, he is delivered of it with pangs; he hesitates, stops in his utterance,
20 and always expresses himself inelegantly. His actions are all ungraceful; so that, with all his merit and knowledge, I would rather converse six hours with the most frivolous tittle-tattle woman, who knew something of the world, than with him. The prepos-
25 terous notions of a systematical man, who does not know the world, tire the patience of a man who does. It would be endless to correct his mistakes, nor would ᵓke it kindly; for he has considered everything

deliberately, and is very sure that he is in the right.
Impropriety is a characteristic, and a never-failing
one, of these people. Regardless, because ignorant,
of custom and manners, they violate them every
moment. They often shock, though they never mean
to offend; never attending either to the general character, or the particular distinguishing circumstances
of the people to whom, or before whom, they talk:
whereas the knowledge of the world teaches one that
the very same things which are exceedingly right 10
and proper in one company, time, and place, are
exceedingly absurd in others. In short, a man who
has great knowledge, from experience and observation of the characters, customs, and manners of mankind, is a being as different from, and as superior to, 15
a man of mere book and systematical knowledge, as
a well-managed horse is to an ass. Study therefore,
cultivate, and frequent, men and women; not only
in their outward, and consequently guarded, but in
their interior, domestic, and consequently less dis- 20
guised, characters, and manners. Take your notions
of things, as by observation and experience you find
they really are, and not as you read that they are
or should be; for they never are quite what they
should be. For this purpose do not content yourself 25
with general and common acquaintance; but, wherever
you can, establish yourself, with a kind of domestic
familiarity, in good houses. For instance; go again
to Orli for two or three days, and so at two or three
reprises. Go and stay for two or three days at a 30
time at Versailles, and improve and extend the

---

²⁹ Orli. Perhaps Orly, a village near Versailles.
³⁰ Reprises. Returns.

acquaintance you have there. Be at home at St.
Cloud; and whenever any private person of fashion
invites you to pass a few days at his country-house,
accept of the invitation. This will necessarily give you
5 a versatility of mind, and a facility to adopt various
manners and customs; for everybody desires to please
those in whose house they are; and people are only
to be pleased in their own way. Nothing is more
engaging than a cheerful and easy conformity to
10 people's particular manners, habits, and even weaknesses; nothing (to use a vulgar expression) should
come amiss to a young fellow. He should be, for
good purposes, what Alcibiades was commonly for
bad ones, a Proteus, assuming with ease, and wearing
15 with cheerfulness, any shape. Heat, cold, luxury,
abstinence, gravity, gayety, ceremony, easiness, learning, trifling, business, and pleasure, are modes which
he should be able to take, lay aside, or change
occasionally, with as much ease as he would take or
20 lay aside his hat. All this is only to be acquired by
use and knowledge of the world, by keeping a great
deal of company, analyzing every character, and
insinuating yourself into the familiarity of various
acquaintance. A right, a generous ambition to make
25 a figure in the world, necessarily gives the desire of
pleasing; the desire of pleasing points out, to a great
degree, the means of doing it; and the art of pleasing
is, in truth, the art of rising, of distinguishing one's
self, of making a figure and a fortune in the world.
30 But without pleasing, without the Graces, as I have

---

13 **Alcibiades.** (B. C., 450-404.) An Athenian of remarkable ability and bad
morals. Socrates tried in vain to win him to a virtuous life.

told you a thousand times *ogni fatica è vana.* You are now but nineteen, an age at which most of your countrymen are illiberally getting drunk in port, at the University. You have greatly got the start of them in learning; and if you can equally get the start 5 of them in the knowledge and manners of the world, you may be sure of outrunning them in Court and Parliament, as you set out so much earlier than they. They generally begin but to see the world at one-and-twenty; you will by that age have seen all Europe. 10 They set out upon their travels unlicked cubs; and in their travels they only lick one another, for they seldom go into any other company. They know nothing but the English world, and the worst part of that too, and generally very little of any but the Eng- 15 lish language; and they come home, at three or four-and-twenty, refined and polished (as is said in one of Congreve's plays) like Dutch skippers from a whale-fishing. The care which has been taken of you, and (to do you justice) the care you have taken of 20 yourself, has left you, at the age of nineteen only, nothing to acquire but the knowledge of the world, manners, address, and those exterior accomplishments. But they are great and necessary acquisitions to those who have sense enough to know their true 25 value; and your getting them before you are one-and-twenty, and before you enter upon the active and shining scene of life, will give you such an advantage over all your contemporaries, that they cannot overtake you; they must be distanced. 30

---

¹ Ogni fatica è vana. Every effort is vain.

Letter LXV

THE VALUE OF METHOD

LONDON, February 26th, 1754.

MY DEAR FRIEND: Now, that you are soon to
be a man of business, I heartily wish you would
immediately begin to be a man of method, nothing
5 contributing more to facilitate and dispatch business
than method and order. Have order and method in
your accounts, in your reading, in the allotment of
your time, in short, in everything. You cannot conceive how much time you will save by it, nor how
10 much better everything you do will be done. The
Duke of Marlborough did by no means spend, but
he slatterned himself into that immense debt, which
is not yet near paid off. The hurry and confusion
of the Duke of Newcastle do not proceed from his
15 business, but from his want of method in it. Sir
Robert Walpole, who had ten times the business to
do, was never seen in a hurry, because he always
did it with method. The head of a man who has
business, and no method nor order, is properly that
20 *rudis indigestaque moles quam dixere chaos.* As you
must be conscious that you are extremely negligent
and slatternly, I hope you will resolve not to be so
for the future. Prevail with yourself only to observe
good method and order for one fortnight, and
25 I will venture to assure you that you will never neglect them afterward, you will find such conveniency

---

²⁰ Rudis . . . . chaos. Ovid, 1, 7. "A shapeless, unformed mass which
we call chaos."

and advantage arising from them. Method is the
great advantage that lawyers have over other people
in speaking in Parliament; for, as they must necessarily observe it in their pleadings in the Courts of
Justice, it becomes habitual to them everywhere else. 5
Without making you a compliment, I can tell you
with pleasure, that order, method, and more activity
of mind, are all that you want, to make, some day or
other, a considerable figure in business. You have
more useful knowledge, more discernment of charac- 10
ters, and much more discretion than is common at
your age; much more, I am sure, than I had at that
age.—Experience you cannot yet have, and therefore
trust in the meantime to mine. I am an old traveler;
am well acquainted with all the by, as well as the 15
great, roads; I cannot misguide you from ignorance,
and you are very sure I shall not from design.

I can assure you that you will have no opportunity
of subscribing yourself, my Excellency's, etc. Retirement and quiet were my choice some years ago, 20
while I had my senses, and health and spirits enough
to carry on business; but now I have lost my hearing, and find my constitution declining daily, they
are become my necessary and only refuge. I know
myself (no common piece of knowledge, let me tell 25
you), I know what I can, what I cannot, and consequently what I ought to do. I ought not, and
therefore will not, return to business, when I am
much less fit for it than I was when I quitted it. Still
less will I go to Ireland, where, from my deafness 30
and infirmities, I must necessarily make a different
figure from that which I once made there. My pride
would be too much mortified by that difference. The

two important senses of seeing and hearing should
not only be good, but quick, in business; and the
business of a Lord-Lieutenant of Ireland (if he will
do it himself) requires both those senses in the highest
5 perfection.   It was the Duke of Dorset's not doing
the business himself, but giving it up to favorites,
that has occasioned all this confusion in Ireland; and
it was my doing the whole myself, without either
Favorite, Minister, or Mistress, that made my admin-
10 istration so smooth and quiet.   I remember, when I
named the late Mr. Liddel for my Secretary, everybody was much surprised at it; and some of my
friends represented to me that he was no man of
business, but only a very genteel, pretty young fellow;
15 I assured them, and with truth, that that was the
very reason why I chose him: for that I was resolved
to do all the business myself, and without even the
suspicion of having a Minister; which the Lord-
Lieutenant's Secretary, if he is a man of business, is
20 always supposed, and commonly with reason, to be.
Moreover, I look upon myself now to be *emeritus* in
business, in which I have been near forty years
together; I give it up to you: apply yourself to it, as
I have done, for forty years, and then I consent to
25 your leaving it for a philosophical retirement, among
your friends and your books.   Statesmen and beauties
are very rarely sensible of the gradations of their
decay; and, too sanguinely hoping to shine on in
their meridian, often set with contempt and ridicule.
30 I retired in time, *uti conviva satur;* or, as Pope says,
still better, " Ere tittering youth shall shove you from

---

30 Uti conviva satur.   Horace, Satires, I. 1, 119.   " As a guest fully
satisfied."

the stage." My only remaining ambition is to be
the Counselor and Minister of your rising ambition.
Let me see my own youth revived in you; let me be
your Mentor, and, with your parts and knowledge,
I promise you, you shall go far. You must bring, 5
on your part, activity and attention, and I will point
out to you the proper objects for them. I own I
fear but one thing for you, and that is what one has
generally the least reason to fear, from one of your
age; I mean your laziness, which, if you indulge, will 10
make you stagnate in a contemptible obscurity all
your life. It will hinder you from doing anything
that will deserve to be written, or from writing anything that may deserve to be read; and yet one or
other of these two objects should be at least aimed 15
at by every rational being. I look upon indolence as
a sort of *suicide;* for the Man is effectively destroyed,
though the appetites of the Brute may survive. Business by no means forbids pleasures; on the contrary,
they reciprocally season each other; and I will ven- 20
ture to affirm, that no man enjoys either in perfection
that does not join both. They whet the desire for
each other. Use yourself therefore, in time, to be alert
and diligent in your little concerns: never procrasti-
nate, never put off till to-morrow what you can do 25
to-day; and never do two things at a time: pursue
your object, be it what it will, steadily and indefati-
gably; and let any difficulties (if surmountable) rather
animate than slacken your endeavors. Perseverance
has surprising effects.   30
I wish you would use yourself to translate, every
day, only three or four lines, from any book, in any
language, into the correctest and most elegant Eng-

lish that you can think of; you cannot imagine how it will insensibly form your style, and give you an habitual elegancy: it would not take you up a quarter of an hour in a day. This letter is so long, that it 5 will hardly leave you that quarter of an hour, the day you receive it. So good-night.

Letter XLVI

EVERY MAN THE ARCHITECT OF HIS OWN FORTUNE *

BLACKHEATH, Aug. 26, 1766.

My Dear Little Boy: Your French letter was a very good one, considering how long you have been 10 disused to write in that language. There are indeed some few faults in it, which I will show you when we next meet, for I keep your letter by me for that pur- pose. One cannot correct one's faults without know- ing them, and I always looked upon those who told 15 me of mine as friends, instead of being displeased or angry, as people in general are too apt to be.

You say that I laugh at you when I tell you that you may very probably in time be Secretary of State. No. I am very serious in saying that you may if 20 you please, if you take the proper methods to be so. Writing well and speaking well in public are the necessary qualifications for it, and they are very easily acquired by attention and application. In all events,

---

* This and the following letter were written to his eleven-year-old godson and adopted heir, Philip Stanhope, son of Arthur Charles Stanhope, a distant relative.

16 As friends. "Faithful are the wounds of a friend."

aim at it: and if you do not get it, let it be said of you what was said of Phaethon,

" Magnis tamen excidit ausis."

Every man of a generous, noble spirit desires first to please and then to shine; *Facere digna scribi vel* 5 *scribere digna legi.* Fools and indolent people lay all their disappointments to the charge of their ill fortune, but there is no such thing as good or ill fortune. Every man makes his own fortune in proportion to his merit. An ancient author whom you 10 are not yet, but will in time be, acquainted with says very justly, " *Nullum numen abest si sit prudentia; nos te Fortuna Deam facimus cæloque locamus.*" Prudence there means those qualifications and that conduct that will command fortune. Let that be your 15 motto and have it always in your mind. I was sure that you would soon come to like voluntary study, and I will appeal to yourself, could you employ that hour more agreeably? And is it not better than what thoughtless boys of your age commonly call play, 20

---

² **Phaethon.** In Greek mythology, son of Helios and Clymene. His father permitted him to attempt to drive the chariot of the sun across the heavens : but the horses left their usual track ; and, to avoid damage to the earth, Zeus killed the driver with a thunderbolt.

³ **Magnis . . . . ausis.** He perished in a great attempt.

⁴ **Every man,** etc. Many will take issue with this remark of Lord Chesterfield, which is not supported by the Latin quotation which follows

⁵ **Facere . . . . legi.** " To do things worthy to be recorded, or to record things worthy to be read."

¹² **Nullum . . . . locamus.** Juvenal, Satires, x. 365. " No power is wanting, if discretion be present : we make thee, Fortune, our Goddess, and place thee in heaven." The word *prudentia*, which Lord Chesterfield translates in the lines following this quotation, has an extended signification. Originally meaning *foresight*, it also means *knowledge, skill, sagacity, practical judgment*, etc. *Numen* is also a word of wide meaning, frequently containing the idea of divine power, or of deity itself.

which is running about without any object or design
and only *pour tuer le temps? Faire des riens* is the
most miserable abuse and loss of time that can possibly be imagined. You must know that I have in
5 the main a great opinion of you; therefore take great
care and pains not to forget it. And so God bless
you. *Non progredi est regredi.*

Letter XLVII

ATTENTION AND DILIGENCE

BLACKHEATH, Oct. 4, 1766.

MY DEAR LITTLE BOY: *Amoto quæramus seria ludo.*
10 I have often trifled with you in my letters, and there
is no harm in trifling sometimes. Dr. Swift used
often to say, "Vive la bagatelle," but everything has
its proper season; and when I consider your age now,
it is proper, I think, to be sometimes serious. You
15 know I love you mightily, and I find but one single
fault with you. You are the best natured boy; you
have good parts and an excellent memory; but now
to your fault, which you may so easily correct that I
am astonished that your own good sense does not
20 make you do it. It is your giddiness and inattention
which you confessed to me. You know that without
a good stock of learning, you can never, when you are

---

² **Pour tuer le temps.** To kill time.

³ **Faire des riens.** To do nothing.

⁷ **Non . . . . regredi.** "Not to go forward is to go backward."

⁹ **Amoto . . . . ludo.** Let us lay aside our play, and talk seriously.

¹¹ **Dr. Swift.** (1667-1745.) Dean of St. Patrick's, Dublin, a noted political
writer, now best known by his "Gulliver's Travels."

¹² **Vive la bagatelle.** Long live jesting.

a man, be received in good company; and the only way to acquire that stock is to apply with attention and diligence to whatever you are taught. The *hoc age* is of the utmost consequence in every part of life. No man can do or think of two things at a time to 5 any purpose, and whoever does two things at once is sure to do them both ill. It is the characteristic of a futile, frivolous man to be doing one thing and at the same time thinking of another. Do not imagine that I would have you plod and study all day long; 10 no, leave that to dull boys. On the contrary, I would have you divert yourself and be as gay as ever you please; but while you are learning, mind that only, and think of nothing else; it will be the sooner over. They tell an idle story of Julius Cæsar that he dictated 15 to six secretaries at once and upon different businesses. This I am sure is as false as it is absurd, for Cæsar had too good sense to do any two things at once.

I am sure that for the future you will attend dili- 20 gently to whatever you are doing, and that for two reasons: the one is that your own good sense at eleven years old will show you not only the utility but the necessity of learning: the other is, that if you love me as I believe you do, you will cheerfully do what 25 I so earnestly ask of you for your own sake only. When I see you next, which shall not be very long, I flatter myself that the Doctor will give me a very good account of your close attention. Good-night.

---

⁴ **Hoc age.** Do this thing: give your undivided attention to the subject in in hand.

²⁶ **The Doctor.** His tutor.